# We Were a Nice Normal Family

## A Memoir of Recovery From C-PTSD and the Trauma of Narcissistic Abuse

Patricia A. Grenelle, PsyD

ISBN 978-1-964143-10-1

Suncoast Digital Press, Inc.
Sarasota, Florida

Printed in the United States of America

*Dedicated to*
*Jennie Shepherd Dunn Beardon*
*(1949-2020)*

# Contents

While this book is based on actual events,
certain individuals, entities, characterizations,
incidences, and locations were changed
to protect the privacy of individuals.

# Preface

I wrote this book for anyone who's ever struggled in their relationships and couldn't quite understand why. If you've lived through childhood sexual abuse and found yourself repeating painful patterns in adulthood—especially in the way you relate to others—I want you to know you're not alone. I have done extensive research and learned some shocking statistics. Indeed, there are more people with similar childhood trauma than most would imagine.

In this book, I include these findings, psychological insights, and practical resources to support your healing journey. But I soon realized that wasn't enough. I needed the courage to do what I'd never done before—to share my own story, so that you might find resonance and hope.

As you read, you'll begin to recognize the symptoms of Complex Post-Traumatic Stress Disorder (C-PTSD). Through your own reflections, I believe this awareness can bring a sense of relief, clarity, and healing.

This book is also a tribute to my sister. She was just seventeen months older than me and suffered deeply from the childhood trauma we endured. Her pain was profound, and much of this story belongs to her, too. I carry her with me in every word.

By sharing these difficult memories, I hope others who've faced similar experiences will feel seen and validated—and will recognize the long-term effects that childhood sexual trauma can have on every part of a person's life. Even if this story isn't your own, perhaps someone close to you—a spouse, sister, or friend—will find comfort and healing simply by being understood.

I also hope this work becomes a call to action: that readers feel moved to stand up, speak out, and support the organizations working to prevent child sexual abuse and to help survivors rebuild. Together, we can bring awareness—and real change.

# We Were a Nice
# Normal Family

> "So, like a forgotten fire, a childhood can always flare up again within us."
> —GASTON BACHELARD

# CHAPTER 1

# NIGHTMARES OF THE NORMAL

My sister's husband Ralph sauntered in and walked directly toward me. At six years old, I was more interested in reading and listening to music than anything else when I had a little free time to myself. Ralph invaded my peaceful corner of our rec room and sat too close. I found his six-foot frame and hefty body somewhat intimidating most of the time, but on this day, I grew extremely anxious as he approached me and seated himself between me and the door. So close, he was nearly touching my leg with his. Then he moved even closer as he smiled and flipped the tassels on the top of my headband. He said, "You look really cute," as he handled my tassels and grinned at me.

I wasn't a bit comfortable with this behavior and wondered what his intentions were, especially because he almost closed me in with his body in the corner of the room. I thought it felt "creepy," which is how such a little girl would describe the sense that her physical and emotional boundaries were being seriously overstepped. His dark eyes were roving across my body, making me feel like I had forgotten to put on clothes. He laughed at the tassels on my headband, and when he touched them, it made me feel foolish for wearing such a thing. He played with my headband ribbons and smiled. I felt embarrassed, nervous, and trapped, but I wasn't sure how to get away from him. I wouldn't look at him. I pretended to continue reading my book. "What are you doing?" he asked.

"I'm reading this book about a girl who —" I started, but he cut me off.

"You look so cute," he said softly. I felt afraid and tried to move away. He said, "What's the matter? Are you scared of me?"

1

When he leaned in closer and his face was right in front of mine, I felt confused. Then he leaned in and kissed me on the lips.

Horrified, I could only echo a line I had heard in an old movie the day before: "You fool."

I scurried past him and fled the room, but this moment—my first kiss—would haunt me forever.

---

My childhood unfolded on a 360-acre Illinois farm, shared with my parents and three sisters: Sarah, ten years my senior, married Ralph in 1968. My sister, Josie, was seventeen months older, and Rene, who was eight years my junior, arrived when my parents thought their family was complete. My parents were simple farm folk with a taste for risqué humor, which added to the normalization of out-of-place sexual innuendos pervasive in our household.

My father worked the land before transitioning to insurance sales when we moved to a small town, where I was able to ride my bicycle all over, which I did constantly. His persistent but frustrating job-seeking taught me the value of education and career stability.

My mother maintained a rigid weekly schedule: Mondays for washing clothes, Tuesdays for baking, Wednesdays for cleaning, Thursdays for errands, Fridays for sewing, and Saturdays for grocery shopping. Sarah and Ralph had their own place nearby, but were constant fixtures in our home, especially on weekends. All in all, I had a sense that we were average—not poor like the people living in the two wooden shacks we often passed by, nor rich like the local banker whose mansion I had seen once, overly decorated with Christmas lights and such. We were a nice, normal family.

It was 1957 when my world began to fracture. At six years old, as the school year drew to a close, I was riding a four-wheeled scooter in the gymnasium, waiting for Ralph to pick me up instead of taking the usual bus home. I was excited when I saw him at the entrance, talking with teachers and the principal. My anticipation turned to confusion when, in his car, he wrapped his arm around me, his long fingers resting on my shoulder in a way that made me squirm inside. *This is like on TV when the boy is driving with his girlfriend*, I thought to myself. I was uncomfortable but too scared to scoot away. He gently squeezed my arm, then relaxed his fingers. Squeeze, release. Squeeze, release. I sat, frozen, not daring to breathe.

Once school was out for the summer, I enjoyed our new home and small town in Illinois, where we had moved. In this quaint little community, I was allowed to ride my bicycle all over, including to the post office and the small grocery outlet that sold candy. On days I felt daring, I rode by the haunted house at the end of the street.

Our new house had multiple additions, having once been used as an in-home beauty salon. The kitchen and living room were spacious, and there was one bedroom on the first floor, just off the living room. There was another small room off the kitchen.

A very large recreational room doubled as my mother's washroom. There was a laundry sink near the door to a hallway. The rec room was paneled on one wall and had linoleum flooring. As the room was separated from the rest of the house, it had a wood-burning stove for when the weather was cold. It was furnished with a couch on one wall next to a record player. I loved using the quiet and private space at that end for reading a book while listening to music. The summertime was particularly comfy in this room because it was so peaceful, with no noises from the neighbors or the outside world. I considered it my own personal sanctuary.

One morning, I put on shorts and a sleeveless summer top, combed my hair, and put on a new headband I thought was pretty. I slipped on my sandals and headed down to the recreation room, feeling free and mellow. I was looking forward to getting back to my book, *A Girl of the Limberlost*. My plan was to read while listening to the Ray Coniff Orchestra, who played a peaceful combination of soft instrumental music, including "The Way You Look Tonight," "As Time Goes By," and "In the Still of the Night." It really helped me to relax, focus on the book's words, and immerse myself in the storyline. I was feeling happy and particularly comfortable.

This was the deeply contented little 6-year-old girl whose privacy was invaded by her sister's husband. This is the scene of the crime where stealing my innocence occurred. This is when and where Ralph, over a decade older than me, stole a kiss, as I described at the beginning of this chapter.

— ◇ —

I did not know until I was an adult and in therapy that every family didn't have a brother-in-law, uncle, or grandfather who was like Ralph. I'd seen articles about children who were sexually abused and I was disturbed by it. When I found out I was one of the statistics, I was dumbfounded. Like a fish living in water, I hadn't realized that my world was not THE world. Living with a pedophile in the family meant never escaping sexual tension, and I became conditioned to consider it normal.

The repeated instances of molestation began at the age of six. Although I never succumbed to Ralph's full-on advances, this continued throughout my childhood, adolescence, and teen years. The constant exposure to a variety of forms of sexually explicit comments and innuendos in my "nice normal family" became part of my own psychological makeup. When I became an adult and should have been able to recognize right from wrong, it was not possible to suddenly become discerning about normal vs. dysfunctional sexual attitudes.

Ralph's physical presence was imposing; six feet tall with well-groomed dark hair, a distinctive sway-backed posture, and a pot belly. His dark, penetrating eyes seemed to look through rather than at you. His behavior at family gatherings was always inappropriate, from crude jokes to intentionally embarrassing comments about women's bodies, even how they might behave in sexual situations. He made off-the-wall comments like, "Does the carpet match the drapes?" which my sister later explained to me meant, "Does the color of her pubic hair match the hair on her head?"

His hands were large, and he routinely touched us girls with his long fingers as he was talking to us. He "accidentally" walked in on us, especially Josie and me, in the bathroom, and his roughhousing during summer water fights often crossed boundaries. He once said to me when I was eight years old, "You're about as sexy as a wet dishrag."

One May evening in 1961, my parents, Ralph, my sisters Josie, Rene, Sarah, and I were all seated in the dining room at a large wooden table that dwarfed the room. The meal was a special dinner to celebrate my 12th birthday, and I had requested fried chicken, mashed potatoes, and cream-style corn. Ralph teased me for eating chicken with a knife and fork. He groaned, "What's wrong with you? You're supposed to eat chicken with your fingers." I didn't bother to try to tell him that I hated sticky or greasy hands.

It never worked to defend myself; his teasing went unchecked (ignored by everyone in my nice, normal family, I might add).

When I was eleven, I started my period, and Mom marked it on the kitchen calendar in a red circle with my initials on it. Ralph had a keen sense of humor, often using it to be vulgar or to intentionally embarrass us girls. He said to me, "I see your period is coming up. You're going to be grumpy next week." He looked at me to see my reaction, but instead of acting ashamed (which I felt overwhelmingly), I pretended I had no idea what he was talking about.

Ralph embodied what I would later come to understand as *misogynistic narcissism*—a toxic combination of self-absorption and contempt for women. His behavior reflected a broader patriarchal system where women faced hostility and harassment simply for existing in a world created by and for men. His actions—the unwanted advances, the sexual comments, the violation of privacy—were textbook examples of misogynistic behavior, made more insidious by his position within our family.

— ◇ —

In 1957, we lived on a quiet Illinois farm, but in the South, the Civil Rights Movement was gaining momentum. The tensions persisted, and the Cold War continued. Adults seemed quite uneasy about what they saw on the evening news, and there was an undercurrent of big-picture fear in every adult conversation I found myself around. As for my own state of mind, I had begun to feel disheartened about who I was and the way my life was unfolding. I didn't know why I felt that way, but it seemed to be growing deeper and darker.

At one point, I felt so alone, and I just didn't want to deal with life anymore. I went to my parents' bedroom and retrieved the pistol from under my father's pillow. I sat on the edge of their bed. It was heavy and the metal felt cold as I gripped it with my small hands. I struggled to lift it up towards my head. I was unsure about which part of my head to aim for. Suddenly, I decided it was not a good idea. I replaced the gun and left the bedroom.

I was not concerned with any outcome or response from family members I just thought they and the world would be better off without me in it.

Also, at that time (I was about seven), I started having nightmares about wild animals fighting. They would all be standing on their hind legs in a circle outside the corner of our house, near the back door. Many nights, I would dream about a lion, a tiger, a bear, and a cougar, all reaching out with their front paws to claw at one another. The nightmares mirrored my feelings of being unsafe, out of control, or overwhelmed by my emotions.

I believe now that my fear of the wild animals represented an internal struggle with the trepidation, trauma, and chaos of something "just outside the door," ready to come in and devour me. It confirmed my feelings of helplessness and isolation. The ferocity and wildness of fighting animals could have symbolized my feelings of being alone in pain, highlighting the sense of abandonment.

When I was eight years old, Fidel Castro took command of Cuba, and the Cold War continued. Popular music was characterized by the rock and roll of artists such as Elvis Presley, Little Richard, and Buddy Holly. The Civil Rights Movement activity was still on every evening's news.

My insecurity had swelled into a tidal wave of unbearable emotions. I wondered if I would have the nerve to use the pistol if I tried again. I decided, instead, to hang myself. I put a belt on my closet door, but I didn't know how to attach the belt to the door, so I gave up. Again, this was a fleeting idea that just came to me, and I thought it would be the answer to how awful I felt about myself.

A few years went by—I was still empty inside, but had not again attempted to escape through suicide. In 1962, the most significant event in the news was when President Kennedy had to deal with the Cuban Missile Crisis, a tense 13-day confrontation with the Soviet Union that brought the world to the brink of nuclear war. A key moment in the Civil Rights Movement was the eruption of violent protests when James Meredith, a young black man, was allowed to enroll and attend the University of Mississippi.

Additionally, 1962 saw the career starts of iconic music artists like The Beatles, Bob Dylan, and the Beach Boys. In the space race, John Glenn became the first to orbit the Earth. We watched popular programs on TV like *The Andy Griffith Show* and *The Dick Van Dyke Show*. Yes, if there had been a snapshot of our living room, you'd see a nice, normal family enjoying the black-and-white TV shows and chuckling along with the laugh tracks.

When I was eleven and Josie was thirteen, we visited Sarah and Ralph for a week during the summer at their home in Iowa.

There was no lock on their bathroom door. There was a tub, but no shower, so the only way to shampoo my hair was to dunk my head under the faucet in the bathtub. Just as I bent over after my bath, Ralph opened the door and started to enter. "Oh, excuse me. I didn't know you were in here." It could have been believable if it had occurred once, but this happened over and over.

One hot summer afternoon, Josie and I wanted to go swimming in a nearby lake, but we were both menstruating. Sarah told us to use tampons. Josie and I looked at each other, knowing that neither of us had ever tried them before. Sarah, the older sister we looked up to, made it seem like "of course" that is what you do when you want to go swimming during your time of the month. Because we were so young and innocent, it was next to impossible to find the correct location to insert it. Sarah took responsibility and inserted one for each of us. I was embarrassed and didn't understand the pain or significance of such an act, as it involved breaking the hymen. Ralph, however, was very aware of the circumstances and offered to help complete the task, which was shameful and humiliating to hear from this older man.

During that same visit, I was reading when Ralph approached me and began trying to unbutton my blouse to fondle my budding breasts. I twisted away and said, "What are you doing?" He stopped when Sarah entered the room. I said nothing.

Looking back, it's as though Sarah meant to put Josie and me in precarious situations with Ralph. I don't understand why she would do that, knowing full well that he was taking advantage of the circumstances. It was as if she were purposefully tempting him by encouraging our presence over long periods of time, and then putting us into untenable situations during our visits.

At the time, since Sarah was my older sister, of course I looked up to her, but there started to be cracks in my admiration of her, and these all had to do with Ralph. For example, I learned that Sarah and Ralph were "swingers." I was appalled. In my pre-teen understanding, I could not imagine any upside to such behavior. I don't know if my parents were aware of it—of course it would never, ever come up in our nice, normal family.

When I was about eleven, Martin Luther King delivered his now-famous "I Have a Dream" speech. Our nice, normal family continued in its many dysfunctional ways as usual. My "dream" was only to escape my emotional and mental anguish. I took a handful of pills, including aspirin and antihistamines. I went to my bedroom and began turning in circles, thinking I would pass out.

However, that didn't happen. I became scared, so I told my parents what I'd done. I couldn't explain why, because I didn't know. No emergency services were necessary because it had already been several hours since I had taken the pills, and to them, I seemed fine. But the next day, my parents took me to a mental health facility where I was to speak to a psychologist. I went along, but because he was a foreigner with a thick accent, I couldn't understand him. Instead of telling him about the sexual abuse, I said nothing. He advised my parents that I was alright and not to worry, stating I just needed more recreation in my life.

*What if?* What if he had more seriously considered the fact that a little girl had intentionally tried to poison and kill herself? Even if she wasn't immediately forthcoming, shouldn't one use their professional expertise and intuition to uncover what was going on with the child? All of us need to remember this today. If there are signs, look behind them, look around them, and if needed, dig under them.

◆

When I was fourteen, my nice, normal family moved from Illinois to Grand Junction, Colorado. I had to get used to a new school and teachers, and to a whole array of students who seemed more mature than I was. A boy said to me, "Look at Mrs. Andrews. She's lopsided today, ha-ha." He was referring to her chest, as one bra strap had evidently given way. Because I was from a nice, normal family, I acted like I didn't know what he was talking about.

The classroom culture was not what I was used to. The boys told sexually explicit jokes and interjected off-color comments during class. One boy said, "It's not true that if you do it a lot, you'll go blind, is it?" Another boy said, "Jamie says, 'When girls masturbate, their boobs grow bigger.'" I ignored them and pretended I didn't know what they were talking about, which earned me the nickname "Neuter." I was embarrassed and thought they were being particularly mean. But I said nothing. I wondered why they would call me such a name, so I looked it up in the dictionary. When I discovered it made reference to having no sex, I was ashamed. It made me feel as if I was somehow different and not as "normal" as my peers.

A young male teacher who taught science had undergone surgery for a cleft palate, which left a noticeable scar on his lip. I thought it made him look sexy. Clueless as to what to do with my feeling of attraction, I teased him excessively during that school year by taping a tack on the underside of his science stool, but I was not present when he sat on it. He drove a Ford Bronco that he thought was the best vehicle in the world. I knew where he parked it and placed a "For Sale" sign on it with his home telephone number. I played a number of childish tricks on him, which I thought were pretty funny. He never directly accused me of any of them. I secretly just wanted a moment of his personal attention.

One day, I followed him into a "staff only" room and sat cross-legged on a high tabletop. I see now that I was obviously flirting, but I didn't realize it at the time. "So…somebody tried to sell your car?"

He laughed. "Some joker put a 'For Sale' sign on it. I took it off," he said as he approached me, sitting on the table. He got within arm's reach of me and hesitated. I thought he was going to embrace me or something, but he didn't. Then he said, "You're not supposed to be in here. We should go." We left the room together. Thank goodness he had the good sense not to respond to my unconscious sexual aggression.

― ◇ ―

Because I was exposed to constant sexual references and innuendos during my formative years, the way I made sense of sexuality was rather complicated. I questioned my beliefs about sexuality, relationships, and consent, which caused me to develop a personal sexual ethic rather than align with societal expectations.

The constant exposure led to desensitization, where sexual references became normalized and less impactful, which often blurred personal boundaries. I wrestled with trust issues and fears of judgment based on my early experiences, which adversely affected my relationships with men. I literally had no clue what a healthy relationship with a man would entail; I certainly didn't learn that in my nice, normal family.

As adults, it's up to us to address healing our childhood wounds and to learn the important life lessons we missed. Through years of therapy since 1975, I have identified those issues and worked through them to develop a healthier outlook and more successful intimate relationships. "Inner work" is the most important investment you can make of your time and efforts in order to recondition your mind and beliefs, making healthy relationships with others and with yourself possible.

As a child, I didn't recognize that my feelings of lack of self-worth or desire to kill myself were related to the depression I felt as a result of my convoluted upbringing. I didn't know anything different.

Josie was born seventeen months before me. Our closeness in age made us lifelong friends as well as sisters. When we were adults, Josie told me, "Ralph would come to my bed almost every night in the room that you and I shared. Your eyes were open, and I thought you were aware of everything that was going on. It began when I was about six and lasted until I was 17 and moved away from home."

No, Josie, I was not "aware." It is likely that I saw it all happen but blocked it out, or dissociated as a coping mechanism. Her revelation was not much of a shock, knowing Ralph, but I felt a wave of sadness and hurt when she finally told me about this. Maybe if we had talked at the time, we could have formed an alliance and either told on him together or at least made attempts to protect one another.

We now know that Ralph was a pedophile. All during his lifetime, he sought out situations that would bring him close to young girls. For example, he volunteered as a coach for girls' sports activities. After Ralph and Sarah had been married about ten years, Sarah called me. "I don't know what to do," she cried. "Every time Ralph takes a babysitter home after we've been out, the girl's mother calls me and says he is molesting their daughter." I didn't know what to say.

I guess when she heard her confession spoken out loud, it really hit her and she started sobbing. It was painful to hear her anguish. "You might want to consider leaving him," I said, "since this seems to be a pattern in his life. It's not likely to stop at this late date."

Sarah added, "Our neighbors and friends are aware, too. We had to leave one town because of his escapades…I don't know what to do." Sarah remained with him until his death in 2025. To my knowledge, he was never reported to authorities, never charged with pedophilia or child abuse.

I knew Josie was much more seriously abused than I had been, but I didn't recognize to what extent until I was an adult and we began talking about it. I don't think our parents ever knew the full scope of it. If they did, it was never spoken of because we were, after all, a nice, normal family. And that secret getting out would simply not fit the narrative.

I felt loved by my parents, but at a distance. I never allowed myself to get close to either my mother or father because I felt guilty and feared that if they knew about Ralph's attention, they would not love me, or love me less.

The desire to commit suicide among individuals who were sexually assaulted as children can stem from a complex interplay of psychological, emotional, and social factors. Flashbacks, anxiety, and a profound sense of helplessness characterize complex PTSD. Survivors may experience overwhelming feelings of shame, guilt, and depression. The emotional burden can feel insurmountable, leading to suicidal thoughts.

"I love romance. I'm a sucker for it. I love it so much. It's pathetic." —
Drew Barrymore

# Chapter 2

# What a Ride

In 1968, I was seventeen and still in high school, and the Vietnam War was raging. I met my future husband on the streets of Salt Lake City while walking with two coworkers, who were also in the city to attend a writing conference. John was one of three young men in a car who stopped and asked us to go for a ride. I said to my friends, "No thanks, you go ahead. I'm going back to the hotel." My friends wouldn't take that for an answer, so I finally agreed. *Let's ride!*

We were paired off immediately, I with John in the backseat of the large sedan. John was a big, tall guy with blonde hair and hazel eyes that sparkled when he talked. They passed beers from the front seat to us in the back. John leaned in suddenly and kissed me, and I kissed him back. As we were drinking, talking, and making out, I found him to be very interesting, intelligent, and a great kisser. It was exciting to have a new friend—maybe even a boyfriend.

Before the night ended, John let me know that he was going into the military and would be leaving soon. That was so disappointing. I feared that if I was out of sight, I would also be out of mind. He took my address and said he would write to me. I wanted to be mature and think nothing of it, but inside, I was aching to hear from him again.

I was surprised to receive a letter from John when I returned home to Colorado. We began exchanging correspondence. Then, there was nothing for several weeks. I was concerned that he had lost interest, but surmised that was typical given the way we'd met. Then he wrote again, two months later, explaining that he had been in military training in the Navy and that he was being sent to a ship assigned to a primary port in Japan.

I had grown even more fond of him through our letters and hated the thought of him being off in the war. Almost every day I learned of another classmate or friend who had been killed in the war and would not,be coming home. It was terribly depressing and made me angry. I worried about John and whether he would return. We continued to write to one another; then, there was a period of a few months where I didn't hear from him.

I continued to live my life, seeking out men and boys to date over the next year. I elected to attend a different high school for my senior year because I didn't want to be known by anyone—I wanted a fresh start with different students. I had experimented with sexuality as a teen, but I was still a virgin. I had decided that it was important to me to have my first sexual encounter be a positive and memorable experience.

My best friend, Callie, was a year older than I and had already left her parents' home to live in a small house. She had red hair and a great sense of humor. On the weekends, we would drive down the strip, where all the teenagers made connections and paired up. We each had certain boys that we would go with routinely if they were available. I had started seeing a football player from another high school. His name was Mike. He was a gentle giant who treated me with respect and dignity. He had dark hair and a smile that wouldn't quit. We met up with each other every few weeks and spent quality personal time together, learning about the birds and the bees. We never went on a formal date, but we enjoyed our rendezvous from 1967 to late 1969. I really cared for him, but only in a physical way. We never had a relationship that was not all about lust.

———————— ◇ ————————

One night, early in 1969, I received an overseas phone call from a man who said John had sent a message via ham radio to relay to me that he loved me. It had been 16 months since our chance meeting, since taking that ride that would change the course of our lives. Over that period, John and I had stayed in touch via airmail for weeks at a time; then, the communication would be sparse again. We continued to profess our love to one another and talked about when he would be released from active duty.

A few weeks later, I received a package from John—a diamond engagement ring. I was surprised, but it felt dreamy. High on romantic love, everything else in my life faded into shadows cast by the bright light of my sudden euphoria. I began to prepare for a home away from my parents with this man, with whom I'd spent only three hours face-to-face. He told me his ship would be in port in Seattle for repairs, and since he couldn't take leave, I planned to drive there to meet him. Yes—in my romance-filled teenage mind, it made perfect sense for me to drive by myself from Colorado to the West Coast to see a boy. *What a ride!*

So, in April of 1970, I drove my Volkswagen Beetle to Washington state without stopping except for refueling. Unfortunately, by the time I had driven to about 50 miles east of Seattle, the engine blew out. The mechanic said I'd thrown a rod right through it. I didn't realize the car needed rest, even if I didn't. It stopped in a wooded location on the interstate. I had to walk down the embankment and crawl through a metal fence to seek help. Luckily, when I found civilization again, it was at a summer boys' camp. They allowed me to use the telephone to call for a tow truck and a mechanic from Seattle. The car was towed the last 50 miles. Thank goodness my father had given me the credit card.

When I arrived in Seattle, I found a motel near Lake Union, where John's ship was in dry dock. Our reunion was awkward at first, as we had only had long-distance letters since that one and only time we met on that fateful night two years before. But we settled down to get to know one another again. Our visit together was sweet and loving, although I remember John getting quite upset about the catcalls from his shipmates when I walked onto the dock near his ship. For me, it was a surprise—first of all, that the men reacted in that way, and secondly, by John's anger over it. I felt comforted to know John was protective and respectful of me.

In May, one month after I arrived in Seattle, we were married. I thought it was a marriage made in heaven due to the circumstances of our chance meeting and because our long-distance relationship had served to fuel (only) the romantic side.

─◇─

Our first apartment was in Long Beach, California, where John was assigned after his ship was decommissioned. I noticed there were no stars showing in the night sky. I thought it very strange, as I didn't realize it was because of the smog layer. Our apartment building, located across the street from the beach, was essentially a retirement home for the elderly, but we secured a one-bedroom apartment there and settled in.

One of the first odd things John said to me was when we were getting ready to go to a function. "I don't want you to wear any makeup."

I said, "Why not?"

"Because you don't need it," he said firmly.

This was followed by him obsessively checking the mileage on our car I had used when he was gone. "Why are there so many extra miles on the odometer?" he asked. "Are you going places during the day or night when I'm onboard the ship?"

"What are you talking about? I go to work and the grocery store. That's it." I soon learned he was not only narcissistic but also extremely controlling.

As a woman coming of age in the 1950s, I found myself constrained by the suffocating social norms of the era. My two driving ambitions—upward mobility and the pursuit of knowledge—clashed with society's rigid expectations, especially those of my spouse. During those decades, men's promiscuity was dismissed as natural behavior, while women faced harsh judgment.

The military was considered off-limits to "wholesome" women. The Secret Service didn't accept female agents until 1971, and the FBI didn't until 1972. A woman's place was firmly in the home: cooking, cleaning, shopping, mothering, and maintaining the household. Divorce wasn't just frowned upon—it was nearly unthinkable. In my family, it was unprecedented.

In 1975, the Vietnam War came to an end, and *Jaws* was the movie everyone was talking about. John and I lived in Colorado near my parents after being married for about 5 years, and the newness of that relationship had waned. John would go out to the bars in the evenings and flirt with women. Similar to when I was a child, I was more interested in finding a comfy spot at home to spend time reading or writing.

On a spring evening in 1975, when Ralph and Sarah were visiting the family, I got a call from Ralph who said, "We're at the Hideout Lounge. Your mom and dad, Sarah, and I came in for drinks and we found John here making time with the women." He paused. "You'd better get down here and make it look on the up and up." He wanted to ensure it didn't appear irregular to Mom and Dad, as that type of behavior would not be acceptable.

I was not about to go out in the late evening to a bar. I just wasn't that interested. I told Ralph, "You'd better tell John to come home and we'll talk."

When John arrived, I asked, "What were you doing there? Did Mom and Dad see you?"

"They saw me. I told them you had a headache and didn't feel like going out tonight," he said.

"Do you think they believed you?" I asked. "Maybe you're interested in the kind of lifestyle that Sarah and Ralph participate in," I said, referring to their swinging, which John knew about.

John blushed and said, "Well…" Then he paused, but finished with, "Why—are you?"

"I don't know," I heard myself say.

I hadn't really considered it. But once I did, I had concerns about how it might affect our marriage. But John was already going out. So, I figured I might as well do it, too.

I told him, "If that is something you want to consider, then I would like to do a little research and see what it's all about," I said matter-of-factly.

"Let's look into it," he said.

For the next two weeks, I perused books about the subject, including wife-swapping, swinging, and open marriages. Together, we learned that it had been growing in popularity since the 1960s, starting during the sexual revolution. It received mixed reviews, with some people saying it was a positive way to be open and honest in loving relationships, while others deemed it morally wrong and destructive to a marriage. Discussing it led to fantasizing about it. Considering this as a potential lifestyle increased our libido—we made love more frequently and it was more robust than it had been before.

We learned that the typical swinging couple was likely to be in their thirties and the man usually had a paunch. Methods included parties, where everybody had sex with everyone in attendance, but at some, there were couples who limited their activity to just one other couple. We discussed it off and on over those two weeks, addressing issues such as jealousy, boundaries, open communication, limits, insecurities, potential health concerns, and expectations of each other.

Then, we decided to give it a try. Since we weren't sure how to participate in such an activity or how to adopt the lifestyle, we agreed to seek additional information from Ralph and Sarah.

"We want to know more about your swinging lifestyle," I said to Ralph when I called him after John and I had decided. It was late spring, and they had left Mom and Dad's house to go home to Iowa.

"What do you want to know?" he asked in what seemed like a sarcastic tone.

"Well," I began tentatively, "We think we want to try it."

"Oh, now you tell us." he said. "Why didn't you let us know when we were just there?"

"We only made the decision recently," I replied. "We both have some vacation time, and we're thinking about coming to see you this summer."

---- ◇ ----

During our visit, Ralph and Sarah set up several rendezvous for us to meet with them and other swinging couples for partying. First, we flew in a small plane, piloted by one of the swingers, to a location about an hour and a half away to participate in a party with four couples. It was strange to see individuals who arrived as couples entertaining people who were not their mates. It made me feel uncomfortable, like we were all "cheating" on one another—openly cheating, but still cheating. But I knew that was supposed to happen and that I was expected to participate, since I had identified myself as a "swinger" by coming. So, I did.

I discovered I was not really emotionally prepared. I experienced some difficulty having to share the men with whom I was paired with multiple women throughout the evening, preferring the men not seek out the other women. After being with a man (a stranger, actually) for even a short time, I felt possessive and a pull to keep his attention on me. I had no apprehensions, however, about who John was with or what he was doing.

I think my societal beliefs about exclusivity and expectations were working against me. I was trying to be two different people—a free-spirit swinger and a moral individual who couldn't accept the premises of this counterculture. Despite spending the next year engaged in this activity, my moral self prevailed, and we gave up that lifestyle in 1976.

Looking back, I am ashamed that I participated in such a vile pursuit. The ongoing exposure to unrestricted sexuality during childhood had long-lasting effects on me. I suspect that part of my initial interest in the activity stemmed from my desire to regain control, which I felt I had never had. Swinging placed me in a position of increased power, which I sought after following a lifetime of being subordinate.

In 1977, despite the societal norms that said a woman shouldn't pursue education or careers, I joined the Army Reserve under the Civilian Acquired Skills Program as an E-3. I drilled with the Communications Company under which I enlisted. Then, I requested reassignment to a Supply Company so I could advance in rank. By the time I was an E-5 in 1978, I had begun working as a full-time, active-duty soldier in Salt Lake City. I found a sense of purpose and strength I never knew existed. I was then promoted and selected as the Personnel Senior Sergeant for the 5th US Army Recruiting Command based in Marin County, just outside of the Presidio of San Francisco, where I worked from the Spring of 1981 until late September 1983.

My marriage continued to deteriorate. We tried various arrangements, each one leaving me feeling more lost and confused about my place in the world. For the first time, I began to question the narrative I'd been living. I realized that the limitations I had accepted weren't just from society or my husband—they were claims I'd placed on myself. The innocent, naïve girl who didn't recognize her own worth began to fade away.

By 1980, the marriage had cycled through various desperate attempts at salvation—including swinging and open marriage—followed by counseling sessions where we pointed fingers at each other for making such choices. John, despite his imposing frame and handsome features, was emotionally stunted for his thirty years. He surrounded himself with teenage boys that he called his friends, built castles in the air with grandiose business schemes, and fought viciously against any attempts at self-improvement, whether for himself or me.

"You're lucky you have me," he said, "because you aren't much of a catch. Most men would look down on you."

"And you spend way too much time talking to your sister," he added. "She's a bad influence on you."

He gaslighted me routinely, which seemed to work well for him because I listened and never argued.

I believed everything he said.

> "I must lose myself in action, lest I wither in despair.
> —Alfred Lord Tennyson

# Chapter 3

# The Choice

"You don't need any college courses. You've already got a decent job. It should be me getting more education, but I don't want to. And you shouldn't either."

John nixed my idea to further my education. It was 1981, and we had gotten back together following my hysterectomy, after which he left me because he wanted to have children. We moved from Salt Lake City to the Presidio of San Francisco, where we were assigned a two-bedroom house located on a hill. The Presidio was a military installation that featured military embankments under the Golden Gate Bridge. We spent many hours going through them for recreation.

I commuted the distance of the Golden Gate Bridge (1.7 miles) to the headquarters in Marin County (about 5 miles) every day, and back to the Presidio at lunchtime, and back across the bridge. After six months, once I got to know some of the other soldiers, we formed a group of three and ran from Fort Baker to the Presidio and back every day for physical training. John said, "You've got to quit running so much. You are looking gaunt." In reality, I was well within the US Army weight standards for my height and had never been in better physical shape.

Our relationship continued to be thwarted by my desires for advanced education and upward mobility as well as the effects of living with a narcissist. I said, "I want to take some college courses." He was completely against that, telling me I should not even want such a thing, He added, "After all, I'm not working, so we couldn't afford it anyway."

There was really no reason to prevent me from pursuing further education. I wondered if it was just because he didn't want me to outsmart him. "You're hanging out with too many people who talk too much about college," he said. "You should pay more attention to me and what I'm doing, and spend more time on our relationship."

My sister, Josie, called just then. We talked routinely every few days. She was living in Salt Lake City and was interested in how my new job was going.

As soon as I hung up, John said, "Who were you talking to?"

"My sister," I said.

"You talk to her way too much. You talked to her yesterday. What's going on, anyway?"

"Nothing," I said defensively.

"You talk to your whole family way too much," he said.

What's wrong with talking to my family? I enjoy sharing what we are doing. Is there something wrong with being close to my family? Of course I did not say any of these thoughts out loud.

I didn't understand at the time, but John was being controlling about my associations with others, which is narcissistic. The term, as we know, comes from Narcissus in mythology, whose only concern was his own reflection in a pond. Whenever John felt I wasn't making him my top priority, he couldn't stand it.

- ◇ -

Living in the San Francisco Bay Area from 1981 to 1983 was a unique experience marked by a diverse range of social, cultural, and political factors. Because we lived on the Presidio, Fisherman's Wharf was quite close. We spent hours visiting it, where the briny scent of the ocean mixed with the rich aroma of clam chowder wafting from a nearby vendor. We watched tourists gather around the bubbling pots, their faces full of anticipation. Seagulls squawked overhead, swooping down to catch an errant fry. We would amble toward a wooden bench, taking in the view of Alcatraz silhouetted against the fading sun while savoring our own bowl of creamy chowder, the warmth comforting against the cool ocean breeze.

We rode our bicycles through the city; streets buzzed with life as we navigated through the throngs of people. Street performers strummed guitars, their melodies mingling with the laughter of children. We passed a tie-dye vendor selling shirts in vibrant colors reminiscent of the 1960s. A couple danced near the pier, and I couldn't help but smile, feeling the contagious spirit of the city. The sound of the cable car bell echoed in the background, a reminder that this was a place that moved to its own rhythm.

After performing personnel duties for the headquarters for two years, the fall of 1982 came around quickly. When I was selected to attend the personnel senior sergeant school in Indianapolis for more training in my field, I was delighted because it meant I would be eligible for promotion. I was excited when I told John my good fortune, "I was selected to attend a military school, which will set me up for advancement."

He said, "Where and for how long?"

"Indianapolis for five weeks."

"I don't want you to go."

"But this is about my career," I argued. "I need to learn more and be able to advance in my Army specialty."

"I would be all alone for too long. I don't want you to be that far away for such a long period of time."

"It is something I am expected to do to enhance my job capability. I know you must understand that."

I wasn't sure if he agreed with me about that, but I was adamant that if the military was paying for me to fly to the Midwest for over a month of training, I couldn't refuse. I really thought John would be okay with me going, once he got used to the idea of me being away and him taking care of himself, which of course he was capable of doing. Just more wishful thinking on my part.

Little more was said about it as I made preparations to go to Indianapolis. Although it was a voluntary school, it was exactly what I needed to advance. I considered what he had said to me about going and determined that he didn't want me to go because he would be lonely, and he didn't want me around other people, out of his sight. That was no justification for me not to get the training I needed, wanted, and deserved. It didn't make sense.

My job was important to me, and I wanted to apply myself and advance in the military. As certain as I was that it would be a good move for me, I still doubted myself. It should have seemed like an obvious choice, but I struggled with it. Am I being selfish and unreasonable? I wasn't sure. According to John, that's all it was.

*"Healing is not linear.*
*It's a journey that unfolds in its own time."*
*—Unknown*

# Chapter 4

# Indianapolis

He knew I was married, but we flirted anyway. We were in Indianapolis, where I was assigned to military housing that resembled a motel, with quads of rooms in each building section. My roommate was the woman who left the position that opened for me at Fort Baker, California. Also in my quad were two men enroute to an assignment, and the master sergeant, Craig, who was the ranking attendee in the class. I felt an affinity and connection with Craig from day one.

He and I got to know each other by walking to and from the classroom together and spending time in the common area of the quad, where we would talk with others attending the course. He was only a year older than I, but so old-fashioned in several ways—he used some kind of cream on his hair, his civilian clothes dated back to his high school days, and he seemed more like my dad than a peer. He said he was separated, had a seven-year-old son, and would be reassigned to Fort Knox, Kentucky, when the class ended. I was always flirtatious, but I was probably more so with Craig because he seemed to appreciate my humor.

"Did you see the size of that mud puddle out in front of our building? It's big enough to go skinny dipping in," I said.

"That's true," he said as he laughed. "I'm ready whenever you are," he joked further. I felt somewhat guilty for egging him on. I knew my husband would not appreciate it.

I routinely checked in with John by telephone. One day, I received a call from him, saying, "I have Bell's palsy, and you have to come home. I went to the doctor, and he said it's because you are gone and that you should return. He said you need to call him."

Needless to say, I was taken aback by this information, which seemed like a ploy to get me to abandon my course and return home. I spoke with his doctor, who told me he thought it actually was caused by my absence. I was disturbed, to say the least, but I had committed to staying until I finished the course. I decided to stay the remaining four weeks, and I admit it wasn't much of a dilemma.

Living independently from my husband was a welcome change. It was freeing in that I didn't have to explain my actions or activities, nor did I have to attempt to adjust my appearance, such as wearing less or no makeup or dressing differently to suit him. And I didn't have to hear how I was less than I should be. I'd known from the time I learned from the credit card company that I was getting a divorce that our marital communication had seriously faltered. But the time away from John helped me to recognize just how controlling he had been.

The class, as a military unit, was required to participate in certain activities, such as marching in a change of command ceremony parade and attending ongoing social functions. Craig and I attended a mandatory hail and farewell social, and we both drank, laughing together about anything and everything.

Craig and I walked back to the quad together, once again giggling about the growing foxhole filled with water. We went to his room to say goodnight. When he kissed me, I responded. The dim light of the room wrapped around us like a soft blanket, muffling the outside world. It was a stolen moment, a brief escape from the lives we had built, and the thrill of it coursed through my veins. I could hear the distant hum of traffic, but at that moment, all I could focus on was him.

He stood by the window, silhouetted against the light, his back to me. I admired the way his shoulders tapered down to a narrow waist and the way he carried himself with an effortless confidence that drew me in. My heart raced; I knew this was wrong, but the magnetism was impossible to resist.

As he turned to face me, our eyes locked, and the air crackled with unspoken promises. I felt a rush of heat as he stepped closer, his presence enveloping me. I could see the intensity in his gaze, a mixture of desire and something deeper, something that made the moment feel both electric and fragile.

"Are you sure you want this?" he asked, his voice low and gravelly. I hesitated for just a heartbeat, weighing the gravity of my choices against the exhilaration of the moment. But in that room, with the outside world forgotten, I nodded, the decision made.

With a gentle touch, he reached out, his fingers brushing against my arm, sending shivers down my spine. I leaned into him, craving the warmth of his body against mine. As our lips met, it felt like a spark igniting—a blend of longing and desperation. The kiss deepened, and I lost myself in the taste of him, the way he held me as if I were the only thing that mattered.

We shed the weight of our lives, our expectations, and our regrets. It was just us–two souls intertwined in a moment that felt both thrilling and dangerous. As his hands explored my body, tracing the curves and contours, I felt alive in a way I hadn't in years. It was a dance of passion and vulnerability, each movement echoing the conflicting emotions that churned within me.

I could hear my heart pounding, a reminder of the life I was leaving behind, even if just for a night. But the thrill of the forbidden made every second feel like a rebellion—a defiance against the mundane. I wrapped my arms around him, pulling him closer as if I could erase the boundaries that separated us from the lives we knew.

As we lost ourselves in each other, the world outside faded away, and nothing else mattered. It was a secret written in the shadows, a chapter I would carry with me long after the night had passed.

I felt guilty on one level, but rather accomplished on another level. After all, John had told me I wouldn't be desirable to anyone else. This act proved I was at least somewhat attractive to other men.

As I was preparing to leave his room, he said, "I love you." I was shocked at this comment because I didn't expect anything from the liaison.

Craig and I spent much more time together and got to know each other pretty well. "I'm going to miss you once class is over," he said. I agreed I would miss him as well. He knew about my unhappiness in my marriage and tried to make me feel better about it by being humorous and cracking jokes. He finally said, "Get off of active duty and come live with me in Kentucky. I'll marry you."

"What do you mean by getting off active duty and going to Kentucky? You make it sound so easy! I can't just do that." We exchanged telephone numbers and said our goodbyes. The thought of getting out of the relationship I was in with John sounded appealing because I was feeling very governed by it and his ways. I didn't want to get off active duty. I loved being in uniform. I wasn't sure what I should or could do.

"Every day may not be good,
but there is something good in every day."
— Alice Morse Earle

# Chapter 5

# The Breakup

John knew. And I knew he knew. But we never talked about me being with another man while away at Army training in Indiana.

Once back in San Francisco in the Spring of 1983, we both simply ignored the "secret" and acted like everything was the same as before. One day, John wanted me to accompany him to a bathhouse, something we had not done before. This was back when San Francisco first became a mecca for gays and many bathhouses had recently opened around the Bay area. The clerk seemed to know and acknowledge him, and viewed me with some peculiar interest. I surmised he had been to the same bathhouse with someone else before me, and I didn't think it was a woman. John insisted that I perform oral sex on him during that visit.

Back in our home on the Presidio, there were moments where it seemed possible John and I could reinvent our relationship and save our marriage. But my awareness level had risen too far. I think both the breathing room and the romantic tryst that my time away provided brought more clarity about the relationship being dysfunctional at its core. I made it clear that we were finished as a couple. "I'm going to be leaving."

"Like hell you are!"

"You'll have to find another place to live because the Army will remove me from the accompanied housing."

John's face grew bright red. The explosion came soon after when he threw an oversized glass ashtray across the room. It shattered against the wall, shards of glass spraying everywhere. His words matched his violence: "I won't let you leave me. I'll kill you before I will allow that!"

The sound of the ashtray shattering changed the atmosphere in the room. It was loud and jarring. And it felt like a bold punctuation mark in an argument and a sudden shift in our relationship. I felt a wild mix of emotions. I was scared for my safety and also felt a deep sadness about the hopeless situation.

It was more than just an ashtray; it was a symbol of everything that had been left unsaid between us, the tension building up to that explosive release. The shattered pieces on the floor reflected the cracks in our broken relationship. I was too stunned to speak. I stood there in silence, the air thick with unspoken words. I could feel the heat of his anger dissipating, replaced by an awkward realization of what he had done.

Our living room, once a sanctuary filled with laughter and long dreamy talks, now felt like a war zone. The debris scattered across the floor was a stark reminder of our fragility. At that moment, I questioned everything I thought I knew about love and anger. How do you navigate the fine line between passion and destruction?

This moment changed everything I had thought about the future. It led me to fear being with him. He was so volatile. As I knelt to pick up the shards, I realized something had to change. We couldn't keep living like this; the ashtray was only the beginning.

We were at an impasse. I didn't know what to do except get to safety, so I left the house and called Craig just ten days after leaving Indianapolis. I went to a pay telephone on the base and charged the long-distance call to our home phone.

"Craig, I don't know what I'm going to do. He's really angry and throwing things and breaking them. I'm afraid he's going to hurt me," I said. "He said he would kill me if I left."

"You know you can't stay there with him, right?" Craig was understanding and compassionate. He said again, "Why don't you come to Kentucky? I'll take care of you." I felt better, just knowing someone cared. I kept the call short and told him I would think about what he said.

When I returned to the house, John said, "You think you're so smart! I've got the name and telephone number of the guy you called in Kentucky. The operator told me when I approved the third-party call."

I was very surprised that once he knew that I was calling another man, he had actually authorized the charge. I said nothing except, "I'm going to bed. It's late, and I have to work tomorrow." John followed me to the bedroom and said, "Alright, let's do it."

I said, "No — I'm not going to have sex with you. I'm going to go to sleep."

"Have it your way. Just remember what I said about trying to leave me."

I felt threatened when he said that and decided I would have to find someplace else to stay until he left the quarters.

―――――――― - ◇ - ――――――――

The next day, in the office, I requested to see the commander. It was noted, but he had a busy schedule and I was told I would have to wait until he was available. I went to work and tried not to think about the mess I'd gotten myself into. Around mid-morning, I went to the mailroom, where there was a more private telephone line, and called Craig.

"I was worried about you when you told me what your husband had said. What are you going to do to protect yourself? You've got to let me help you." Craig sounded sincerely concerned.

"I don't know. I've requested to speak to the commander, but I don't know what he'll say. I know I can't continue to stay at the house, in fear for my life. I guess I'll have to go to a motel until I can get John to leave."

"Alright," Craig agreed. "Promise me you'll get a room."

"I will, and I'll check in with you when I do." I felt reassured I had a sound resource to go to for help.

The commander finally called me in at the end of the workday. He said, "Sit down. Tell me what's on your mind."

"Well, Sir, I'm in a situation," I stammered. He waited for me to say more. "My husband is threatening to kill me because I want to leave him."

"You have found someone else." He said it as a statement of fact.

"Yes, Sir, I have," I said hesitantly. "And I'm afraid of him and that he will make good on his promise if I stay here." I waited a moment, then added, "I have a safe place to go if I could get off active duty."

"I'm sorry this is happening to you, but if it's any consolation, these threats generally don't come to fruition." *I wasn't so sure of that.* The commander continued, "If you are sure that's what you feel you need to do, I will take it under consideration and let you know by the end of the week."

"Yes, Sir. It's what I think I should do," I responded with wet eyes because I really liked my job, I was good at it, and I really wanted to stay.

For the next several days, I stayed in a motel. I let Craig know I was safe and he asked me what the commander had said about me leaving active duty. "He'll let me know by close of business on Friday," I explained. "He told me that those types of threats generally don't materialize, but I hate to take that chance!"

"You need to come here and be safe with me," Craig said, and added, "Soon."

I explained that even if I was authorized to leave, I would have to clean and clear quarters first.

"I know, but you should be able to do that quickly," he said encouragingly.

Next, I called John and said, "I'm not coming home. You need to collect your stuff and vacate the house. I'll need to turn over the quarters back to the Army."

"Where are you?" he demanded to know.

"I'm in a safe place. If you don't pack up and leave, the military police will assist you." I didn't know that for sure, but it sounded reasonable.

He hung up on me.

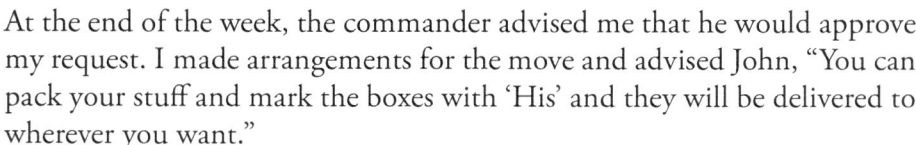

At the end of the week, the commander advised me that he would approve my request. I made arrangements for the move and advised John, "You can pack your stuff and mark the boxes with 'His' and they will be delivered to wherever you want."

"Please come home. We should talk," he begged.

"No," I responded, "I believe we've said it all." I didn't want to give him any more opportunity to threaten me or to carry out his promise. My eyes burned with tears, but I didn't let him know that. I knew I had to be strong and not go near him despite my overwhelming feelings of grief and loss for our dead relationship.

John left two days later, leaving a note on the kitchen table for me. It simply said where to send his belongings, which was to his mother's house in Salt Lake City. I was watching the house from afar, and I saw John load up his car and leave the quarters. I went to see what shape the house was in. He'd gone without doing any cleaning or yard work. Unfortunately, due to his incessant smoking, the walls needed to be scrubbed clean of serious dirt and grime. It took me three weeks to get the place in order. I moved to the barracks during the interim.

As I packed the rest of my own belongings, I looked for the silver certificate dollar bill that my uncle had won on the day I was born, at the 1951 Kentucky Derby, 32 years prior. It was gone. The card that had explained its origin was nowhere to be found. I sat down and cried.

— ◇ —

Domestic violence may have been more prevalent in that era than today, I'm not sure. I just know I didn't hear much about it, and considering my own intense shame, I can see why it was kept quiet in far too many homes, especially in those of the "nice, normal family." Let's look at some current statistics.

According to the CDC, domestic violence remains a significant issue both in the United States and worldwide, impacting millions of individuals each year through physical, sexual, emotional, and psychological abuse. Current Statistics on Domestic Violence in the United States (2025): Over 12 million men and women experience intimate partner physical violence, stalking, or rape each year, equating to about 24 victims per minute in the U.S.

According to the World Health Organization (WHO), approximately twenty-nine percent of women and ten percent of men in the U.S. have experienced rape, physical violence, or stalking by a partner that has adversely affected their daily functioning. Nearly fifteen percent of women and four percent of men have suffered injury due to intimate partner violence, which includes physical violence, sexual violence, or stalking.

Each day, over 20,000 calls are made to domestic violence hotlines in the U.S., indicating a substantial ongoing need for support services. Emotional abuse includes behaviors such as humiliation, insults, threats, controlling actions, and gaslighting, which aim to control and dominate the victim.

The mental health impact is huge: victims often endure significant mental health consequences, including moderate to severe symptoms of Post-Traumatic Stress Disorder (PTSD) and depression, especially when abuse includes multiple types such as physical violence, sexual coercion, psychological abuse, and stalking. The co-occurrence of these abuse forms worsens the psychological impact on victims, highlighting the complexity of domestic violence and the importance of comprehensive interventions.

—◇—

Why do people put up with living in fear? Why did I tolerate it for *any* amount of time? "Attachment Theory" identifies several types of attachment styles that describe how individuals relate to others in close relationships. These styles generally stem from early interactions with caregivers and can influence interpersonal relationships throughout life. Here are four:

**Secure Attachment**:—Individuals with secure attachment feel comfortable with intimacy and independence. They trust others easily, seek out support when needed, and have healthy self-esteem. They are good at communicating their needs and emotions.

**Anxious-Preoccupied Attachment**:—This style is characterized by a strong desire for closeness and intimacy, often accompanied by anxiety about partner availability and fear of rejection. Individuals may appear clingy or overly dependent on their partners for emotional support and validation.

**Dismissive-Avoidant Attachment**:—Individuals with this attachment style tend to prioritize self-sufficiency and independence, often avoiding emotional closeness. They may have difficulty expressing feelings, can seem emotionally distant, and often downplay the importance of relationships.

**Fearful-Avoidant (or Disorganized) Attachment:**–This style blends aspects of both anxious and avoidant attachments. People may want closeness but also fear it, causing them to act in conflicting ways. They might have trouble trusting others and often have a chaotic approach to relationships, usually rooted in past trauma or inconsistent caregiving.

"People who lack solid early attachment bonding to a primary caregiver, and therefore lack a foundation of safety, are much more vulnerable to being victimized and traumatized and are more likely to develop the entrenched symptoms of shame, dissociation and depression." (Peter A. Levine, *In An Unspoken Voice: How the Body Releases Trauma & Restores Goodness*).

Understanding these attachment styles can help individuals and therapists identify patterns in relationships, leading to healthier interactions and improved emotional well-being.

"Out of the ashes we rise,
stronger and more determined."
—Unknown

# Chapter 6

# Craig

"What the hell am I doing?" I asked, talking out loud to myself to help me stay awake on the long, grueling drive. When I arrived in Kentucky, I was exhausted from the trip and unsure of how Craig would receive me. It had taken me four weeks to tie everything up, leave, and make our rendezvous. It was the fall of 1983, and Craig had been assigned to a barracks building on Fort Knox, where he let me stay with him. It was for single soldiers and was antiquated. There was only a single twin bed, which we shared.

It was certainly not the most glamorous way to live, but it was a safe roof over my head. I did not know what to expect in the flurry of moving to Fort Knox, and I was experiencing some culture shock.

"Here is some wine to celebrate your arrival," Craig offered, holding out a plastic goblet. I imbibed until I was sufficiently drunk, then I vomited and had dry heaves because I had not eaten anything for hours.

Craig asked, "Are you okay? Here, I brought you some peaches." He gave me a bowl of canned fruit and a spoon. I sat up from lying on the bed and ate them.

We lived together in the barracks for two weeks, and then Craig said, "My name finally came up for the apartment I applied for. We can move in there tomorrow." It was a one-bedroom, furnished apartment on the ground floor of a newer apartment complex in Radcliff, Kentucky.

When I met Craig, he had told me he was separated, but he didn't explain that it was only geographically and really due to the miles between his "ex" in Texas and wherever he was stationed. He was not "legally separated," and

I wondered if his wife had a clue about his "it's all over" attitude toward their marriage.

"I don't want you to work outside the home," he told me. "I want you to stay home and be a housewife."

I said, "We'll see." It seemed strange that he didn't want me to work outside the home, but I let the idea pass and said nothing.

We had lived together for 45 days when he announced his plan to take vacation time to go see his wife (his "ex," according to him). I asked, "Why do you need to go see her in Texas?"

He said simply, "Because she asked me to."

I began drinking, then I went to the club on base and drank some more. Craig followed me to the club and said, "I don't know why you're so upset about this."

"Because you told me you were separated and I believed you!" I sat at the bar where he ordered one drink, standing next to me.

Then he said, "We had just split when I moved from Alaska to Fort Knox after the military training in Indianapolis, and she moved to Texas."

"So, you're not legally separated then," I asked, dumbfounded at my naivety. Just then, the bartender started to take notice, so Craig moved away from me towards the entrance to the club so as not to cause a scene.

"I'm going to drive there tonight. It's already late. I need to leave." He walked out the door.

I finished my drink and followed him to the apartment, where he was packing his bags. "Do you need to leave right now?" I asked him in a drunken stupor. I fell to my knees on the bathroom floor, lay down, and rested my face on the cool tile. It felt good. In my fog, I heard Craig walking away but I couldn't get up.

Craig left me there on the floor and went to Texas.

———— ◇ ————

*What the hell am I doing?* I asked myself, wondering what future plans would look like with Craig. After all, I was 33 years old, and obviously, I didn't know. The more I interacted with Craig, the more I began to have concerns about who he really was and what he was about. I needed to know whether we had a life together. And Craig didn't seem forthcoming. I worried and wondered, *What other mistruths or lies has he told me? Is this just the beginning of a long line of misperceptions and poor communication?*

After ten days, Craig came back to the apartment and tried to act like nothing had occurred between us. I was emotionally distant and physically avoided him. He said, "What's the matter with you?"

"You left me on the bathroom floor. You didn't know if I was going to be okay or not."

"I was pretty sure that you'd be okay once the liquor wore off," he faltered, then said in a complaining tone, "I tried to have sex with her, but I couldn't," he whined. I didn't know what to think of that. The fact that he tried told me there was still some desire there. I didn't know how to respond to his comment.

Then he quickly changed the subject. "There is a ballgame on this afternoon. Let's do popcorn and beer and lie on the living room floor and watch it there."

"That's all you've got to say for yourself after leaving me like that?"

"Oh, come on," he said with an exaggerated pout. "Don't be angry with me."

I felt horribly disregarded and disrespected, but I yielded to him and we continued to live together, although I was far away from him in many ways.

His preference for me not to work no longer had the weight it once did with me. I went to work at Fort Knox at the US Army & Armor School Publication Warehouse as a supervisor with four employees, including a clerk-typist and three warehouse workers. I was responsible for ordering and maintaining all US Army publications necessary to operate the Armor School and Fort Knox. This required special training and knowledge of supply and demand, which I had learned as a Reservist after my active duty ended. Rocky, my warehouse supervisor, was a good-looking 28-year-old guy whom Craig had some issues with, accusing me of being too friendly.

One night in the winter of 1983, Craig didn't come home until very late, and when he did, he was drunk. He lay down on the couch and started to stiffen like he was going to have a seizure. I walked over to him and asked, "Are you okay?" He rose up off the couch and punched me square in the stomach. I fell backward and caught myself from falling on the floor.

*Who is this man?! How can he be so mean?* I was beside myself with hurt and confusion. I tried to help him, and he struck out at me.

*Why is he doing this? What is wrong with him?*

At first, I thought I'd need to go to urgent care and be seen, but I decided against that and gathered a few personal items and my purse and left as fast as I could. I checked into a local motel. This erratic behavior dumbfounded me, but I decided he was never going to lay another hand on me.

My motel room was located on the second floor, featuring a balcony area at the front. In the morning, I walked out onto the balcony and noticed him in his truck cruising the parking lot looking for my car. "Come talk to me," he yelled out the window of his truck as soon as he saw me.

"Why should I do that?"

"Just so we can talk," he said.

Against my better judgment, I came downstairs and got inside the truck in the passenger seat. I looked at him, expecting him to start talking. "Well, what have you got to say for yourself?" I asked pointedly.

"Just that I got really drunk," he began. He paused and continued slowly, "I lost my job last night. They removed me from my position as First Sergeant," he said, sounding so pained, and as though he expected me to be consoling.

"So why did you hit me?" I asked.

"I didn't know what I was doing," he said. Then he added, "I don't remember hitting you." We were silent for a moment. "Can we just go home?" he pleaded.

I stared at him, then said, "That will never happen again. Do you hear what I'm telling you?"

He didn't say anything but nodded in compliance. I would have liked to have had more discussion about the entire situation, but he wasn't up for it. I got out to go gather my belongings, got into my own car, and followed him to the apartment.

I considered my future with Craig. After many days and sleepless nights, I decided I should leave him and go back on active duty. I learned the only way that could happen was to apply for Recruiting Command as a recruiter. I put in my application, which required an official Army photograph, but

I was never called for an interview. Perhaps it was my photo, in which I appeared slightly unkempt. My hair needed to be styled, and my look was just not STRAC enough. It looked as though I had been roughed up, which I guess I had.

Craig had little to say about my applying for active duty. He didn't seem to be particularly for it, but he never said anything against it.

---

In the spring of 1984, *The Terminator* and *Beverly Hills Cop* were on the big screen, and the most popular ad on television was an older lady standing at a burger counter, demanding, "Where's the beef?" After we watched Indiana Jones duke it out, Craig said to me, "Let's buy a house."

Together, we purchased a three-bedroom home on a hill in Elizabethtown, Kentucky, close enough to Fort Knox to hear night-firing maneuvers. It had a partially finished basement. We worked together to finish it by putting down ceramic tiles we bought at a wholesaler. It looked good. We were proud of our accomplishments.

On one side of the house was a large area of weeds and brambles. I tackled it with a lawn mower that bottomed out numerous times, but the area looked great when I was done. The neighbors appreciated my efforts. Craig said nothing.

We continued our daily routine of going to our jobs and coming home to put in more work in the house. We had over an acre of land, much of which had trees, where Craig wanted to put in a picnic area, and he did.

On my birthday, I expected an engagement ring. On Christmas and then on Valentine's Day, I expected an engagement ring. Each time I received a small box, I was anticipating something more substantial, but it never arrived. A necklace, a bracelet…no ring. I was heartbroken and devastated because of the fact that he had promised to care for me, and I completely believed that what he meant was marriage.

But that was not happening.

---

Warning: rape scene. It was the Fall of 1985, and Craig and I had lived in the house for almost a year. We had shared laughter and quiet moments where the walls of our home bore witness to both tenderness and tension. One evening, Craig said, "I'm going out."

That night, I felt a confusing mix of trust and apprehension, a blend as the evening unfolded. It was a Saturday night, and Craig started ranting about men and women not being complementary to one another as he walked through the house in what seemed like a manic state.

He kept talking as he walked from one room to another, collecting bits and pieces of himself, his wallet, keys, etc. I followed him from room to room, trying to understand what he was going on about.

Craig suddenly grabbed me and threw me down onto the bed in our bedroom. I tried to get up, but he was too strong. My recent sense of safety vanished and was replaced by fear and disbelief. Because what happened next shattered my sense of security. I found myself trapped in a reality I couldn't escape.

He tore my jeans off of me. I screamed, "What the hell are you doing?" Then I just screamed. He grabbed my panties and yanked them down to my ankles. Feelings of helplessness washed over me like a cold wave. I was drowning in humiliation. It was incredibly dehumanizing, the way he forced himself into me repeatedly.

Afterward, he put himself back together and left the house. I was dumbfounded by the level of aggression, force, and anger he expressed. That wasn't sex; that was a violent outburst of controlling behavior. The kind of brutality women have suffered since the dawn of humanity.

In the days that followed, I grappled with confusion and shame, questioning my own judgment and the authenticity of my past happiness over the last year or so. I knew that research shows such behaviors can be driven by dominance, control, and revenge. I wasn't sure what his reasoning was—if there actually was any —but it was not acceptable, regardless. My trust in Craig was destroyed. I never again felt comfortable around him. Even when he was on his best behavior, there was always a question about his genuineness.

I couldn't believe he'd done that and with such abandon. He'd morphed into a monster right before my eyes. As soon as he left, I locked the door.

I was fearful he would return and kill me. I collected my belongings and drove to town to locate an apartment to rent. I was relieved to find one that day that I could occupy the very next day.

Craig came in extremely early the next morning, very drunk. He went to bed. He said nothing to me until later in the day when I announced, "I'm moving out."

"To where?"

"I've found an apartment in Radcliff."

"When?" he asked, rather sullenly.

"Today. I just need to gather a few more things, and I'm ready."

"Where is this apartment?" he asked.

"In Radcliff," I said, to put him off. I collected the rest of my personal items and left. He just watched me go. He said nothing.

───── ◇ ─────

My furnished apartment was a one-bedroom with a broken heater. That month there was an ice storm, and it was insanely cold. I located another apartment and moved slightly further out of town.

I started seeing other men. Craig found out where I had moved and began calling and asking me out, which I declined. Before the rape, we had planned a spring trip to Las Vegas, but I had since canceled it.

He called me in the spring of 1986 when he learned he was being reassigned to Germany for the last two years of his active-duty period in the Army. He finally confessed to me that he had promised his ex that he would not marry anyone for two years after they had been legally separated. That was when he requested the divorce be finalized. So, when he told me to come to Fort Knox, he hadn't been free to marry, in addition to being still virtually committed to his ex. It confirmed to me that he was a pathological liar. He said whatever he could get away with. To hell with the truth.

Craig began preparing to permanently transfer to Germany by putting the house up for sale and closing out all ties to Fort Knox, as I stayed in my apartment in Radcliff.

I continued to work as the Publications Supervisor. When word got out at Fort Knox that I had split with Craig other men showed an interest in getting to know me. Unfortunately, many of the interested suitors were married.

Rocky was kind to me during this phase of my life. We talked about Craig and how relationships change. He had gotten married in the interim and said, "I'm learning about the ups and downs of married life." He was a good friend and a source of platonic comfort for me during this difficult time.

Craig was aware that I was seeing other people. He showed up at the Publication Warehouse one day with the Willie Nelson recording, "You Were Always on My Mind," which we had considered our song because it seemed like there was a pattern of behavior in which he 'didn't treat me quite as good as he should have and never told me he was happy that you're mine.' When he asked me to dance with him to that song, it felt like he was trying to make amends for the horrible way he had treated me. My first reaction was absolutely not, but then I reconsidered because he was being reassigned overseas and I thought it might be a way for us to depart at least in a friendly manner. I hesitantly accepted his hand and we danced.

Looking back, I'm astounded that I was willing to even be in the same room with him after the way he had treated me. We danced. It was just okay. It didn't garner any new feelings of love or enchantment. We talked briefly about his upcoming transfer, then he left.

---

The Centers for Disease Control (CDC) estimates that between 10% and 14% of women experience marital rape. One study found rapes committed by husbands or ex-husbands were four times more common than rape by strangers.

Intimate partner rape, according to the CDC, is found to affect one in three female rape victims (more than thirty-nine percent). Over one in eight male rape victims (over twelve percent) were raped by an intimate partner.

If you are experiencing intimate partner violence, including sexual assault or coercion, help is available by reaching out to one of these resources:

- **The National Domestic Violence Hotline**: 1-800-799-SAFE (7233) or text START to 88788. (http://www.thehotline.org)

- **The National Sexual Assault Hotline (RAINN)**: 1-800-656-HOPE (4673) (https://rainn.org)

- **StrongHearts Native Helpline**: 1-844-7NATIVE (762-8483) (https://strongheartshelpline.org)

- **Love is Respect**: Text "Lovels" to 22522 or call 1-866-331-9474 (https://loveisrespect.org)

- **Victim Connect:** 1-855-4VICTIM (855-484-2846) (https://victimconnect.org)

- **The Network/La Red**: 1-800-832-1901 (for LGBTQ+, kink, and polyamorous individuals) (https://tnlr.org)

- **The National Human Trafficking Hotline** 1-888-373-7888; TTY: 711; Chat: Text 233733 (https://humantraffickinghotline.org)

"The strongest people are those who
win battles we know nothing about."
—Unknown


# CHAPTER 7

# LAS VEGAS


In May of 1986, Craig showed up at my apartment and insisted I go with him to the travel agency to buy his ticket to Las Vegas.

I said, "No. I don't want to ride with you."

"Come on," he pleaded. "The least you can do is accompany me just this once. Then we'll go out for dinner."

I was hesitant, but since he offered to pay for dinner, I accepted.

At the travel agency, he informed the clerk that I had been scheduled to go to Las Vegas, but had backed out.

She said, "Oh, come on. You need a vacation from this place, too." She was just being friendly, but I didn't appreciate her input.

I said, "No, I'm not going. Thank you anyway."

Then both the clerk and Craig started trying to convince me. I held firm. "No, I'm not going."

"Come on," said Craig. "I'll not only pay for your ticket, but I'll throw in $100 for you to gamble with." He had always been quite a tightwad, so this got my attention.

When I hesitated, he said, "All right, $200 extra then."

I was weakening in my resolve. Finally, I said, "All right. You've convinced me." He bought our tickets to Las Vegas and we went out for dinner.

—◇—

It was June of 1986 when we took a morning flight to Las Vegas, which was uneventful except that we started drinking on the plane, which was the beginning of a long period of steady alcohol consumption.

We stayed at the Imperial Palace. The ambiance was vibrant and colorful, capturing the essence of the era's fascination with glitz and glamour. As we stepped into the busy hotel lobby, the air buzzed with excitement, and a palpable energy mirrored the flashing lights of the casino floor. The scent of fresh popcorn mingled with the musky aroma of cigars, creating a unique blend that was both intoxicating and overwhelming. Everywhere I looked, there was a kaleidoscope of colors—neon signs flickered overhead, casting a surreal glow on the guests who wandered through the opulent lobby.

Clinking coins, the cheerful clanking of slot machines, and laughter danced through the air like music. In every direction, the clatter of chips being exchanged at card tables intertwined with the distant strains of live entertainment, a constant reminder of the vibrant nightlife for which Las Vegas is famed.

Guests moved with a sense of purpose, their attire a mix of sequins and sharp suits, embodying the glamour of the time. The overall atmosphere was a curious blend of thrill and excess, where dreams felt attainable amidst the shimmering chaos.

The decor spoke of a bygone elegance, with plush carpets featuring bold patterns and ornate chandeliers hanging from the ceilings like jewels. The walls were adorned with murals that depicted scenes of classic Vegas, capturing the spirit of a city that thrived on fantasy and indulgence. So, so romantic.

As I wandered through the casino, I could feel the pulse of the place, an undercurrent of hope and desire, as people chased after fortune and fun. It was a world that felt larger than life, a playground for those seeking adventure, and I was swept up in its intoxicating embrace.

We both began drinking as soon as we had checked in and put our luggage in the room. Craig went to play craps, and I sought out the Blackjack table, both of which kept the alcohol flowing. We agreed to meet for dinner at the hotel's Emperor's Buffet at 6 pm.

Once seated for dinner, we had drinks before, during, and after we ate. Craig said, "And just think, you almost passed all of this up."

"Yes, I almost did," I replied flatly. "What shall we do after dinner?"

"I don't know. I was thinking maybe we should check out the hotel wedding chapel," he said, slurring his words.

I laughed. "That would be something, wouldn't it?" I was being facetious. I thought he, too, was joking.

"I guess we could get married and if it didn't work out, we just get a divorce," Craig suggested.

"Oh, just get a divorce, huh? You make it sound pretty cut and dry." At that time, I didn't know Craig had been married three times already, and I was so inebriated that it likely wouldn't have made a difference to me had I known.

I was torn by what he was suggesting. For the last two years, this was what I had expected, wanted, and anticipated. But now it didn't feel right.

"Well, yeah. That's what we'd do," he declared.

I was also so drunk it didn't dawn on me that this was not only a pre-nuptial agreement, but it also meant we'd be lying about promising to love, cherish, honor, and obey one another until death do us part if we planned on divorce if it didn't work out.

We had one more drink and discussed his upcoming move to Germany. He said, "You can go with me, but on an unaccompanied tour, because I don't want to incur three more years before I can retire."

We walked to the back of the hotel to the "We've Only Just Begun Wedding Chapel." A young woman greeted us and we were suddenly planning our wedding. The clerk was so matter-of-fact, it felt like we were renting a car.

The clerk arranged for us to get our license the following morning with a limousine ride to the Clark County Courthouse in downtown Las Vegas. I couldn't believe the swiftness of all that happened. The ride to the courthouse was quiet. We said little to each other during the trip. I think we both had second thoughts about what in the world we were planning to do.

Was this really happening? We were on our way to get married. As I settled into the plush leather seats of the limousine, the scent of rich upholstery enveloped me, a heady mix of sophistication and comfort. The doors closed with a soft thud, cocooning me in a world separate from the bustling chaos of the Las Vegas Strip. The dim ambient lighting inside the car created an intimate atmosphere, contrasting sharply with the bright neon lights outside.

The ride was both intriguing and surreal. As we veered away from the Strip, the scenery shifted. The towering hotels gave way to the more subdued architecture of the courthouse area. The contrast was striking. The imposing facade of the Clark County Courthouse loomed ahead, a stark reminder of the serious business that awaited me. The luxury of the limo felt like a protective bubble, momentarily shielding me from the gravity of the destination. Once again, I was so caught up in an intensely romantic scene that all rational thinking had abandoned me.

Arriving at the courthouse, the driver smoothly pulled to a stop. As the door opened, a rush of city sounds flooded in, and I took a moment to gather my thoughts. The transition from the fantasyland of the Imperial Palace to the solemnity of the courthouse was jarring. I stepped out into the bright Nevada sun, feeling both the weight of anticipation and the lingering echoes of the Las Vegas nightlife behind me.

Getting the license was as routine as signing a check after eating dinner. Back at the hotel, a strange sense of detachment washed over me as I stood amidst the flurry of wedding planning activity. It was as if I were watching a movie, the bright lights and bustling crowd creating a scene I felt barely a part of, yet was intoxicated by.

---

I wore a light blue street-length dress with puffed sleeves and Craig wore a light blue leisure suit. As I walked down the aisle, I could hear the music playing, the soft rustle of fabric as my dress surrounded me, but it all felt dreamlike. Every little detail—the floral arrangements, my bridal bouquet, the large white bows at the "alter," the carefully curated playlist—seemed to swirl around me in a vibrant haze. The words "I do" echoed in my mind, but they felt like a script I was rehearsing rather than a life-altering promise I was about to make. The weight of the moment was immense, yet my heart raced with both excitement and apprehension. I couldn't shake the feeling that this was all happening to someone else.

When the wedding was over, we sat down for dinner. The table was beautifully set, candlelight flickering against the polished surface, yet I felt strange. Laughter floated all around me, but I found myself grasping for any sense of joy, my heart heavy with the weight of our hasty vows.

We ordered drinks and an assortment of dishes meant to celebrate our union. Each bite was a reminder of the sweetness I craved but couldn't quite put my finger on. I forced smiles, nodding along to stories that felt too bright against the murkiness of my thoughts. Was this how it was supposed to feel?

After dinner, we made our way to the casino. It should have been exciting, but instead, I felt almost numb and like an observer of my own life. I watched Craig, his eyes sparkling with hope and anticipation at the craps table while I stood on the sidelines.

I took a place at the Blackjack table and lost myself in the rhythm of the game. It was as if the act of gambling could somehow distract me from the chaos swirling inside. I tried to engage, to match the enthusiasm of the other players, but each win felt hollow, each loss a reminder of the uncertainty that loomed over me.

By the time we turned in early, the weight of the night pressed heavily on my chest. I lay awake, staring at the ceiling. I felt reality creeping in, quieting the hum of the casino that still echoed in my mind. I was married now, but the question lingered: how do I find my footing in a life that, although I had anticipated it for two years, had suddenly been thrust upon me unexpectedly in a weekend? The spectacular wedding show was over. Now it was just the two of us, alone in a space that felt both intimate and foreign.

We had shared fleeting moments of passion throughout our relationship, but this felt different—loaded with significance and pressure. It was supposed to be magical, the culmination of our vows, yet as we began to explore each other, I couldn't shake the feeling that something was off.

The kisses were tender, but they felt hesitant, as if we were both navigating uncharted territory. My mind raced with thoughts, wondering if I should feel a deeper connection, a spark that would ignite the night. Instead, there was an awkwardness that crept in, a disconnect that left me feeling more like a participant in a ritual than a lover in a passionate embrace.

I tried to shake off the nagging feeling of self-consciousness. I wanted to be present, to lose myself in the moment, but the reality was that our bodies felt out of sync. There was a clumsy rhythm to it all, a series of movements that didn't quite match the romantic fantasies I had conjured in my mind. It was as if we were both trying to find our footing on a dance floor where the music had suddenly stopped.

In that moment, I realized that this night—this sacred act of consummation—wasn't going to be the fairy tale I had envisioned. As the night wore on, we found our way back to each other, the intimacy growing slowly, like a flickering flame finding its strength. It wasn't the grand finale I had imagined, but it was ours—an imperfect beginning to a lifelong journey. And maybe, just maybe, the beauty of it lay not in perfection but in the moments of vulnerability and connection that would shape our story. I felt a touch of optimism return.

The next morning, as we prepared to leave, I picked up my lovely bridal bouquet and looked at it, trying to decide what to do with it.

Craig said in an irritated tone, "What the hell are you doing? We need to pack, and you can't take that with you. Just leave it."

I was surprised at his indignant demeanor, "I hate to do that. It's so pretty." I lifted it off the air conditioning unit, where I had placed it to stay cool, so the flowers wouldn't wilt.

"You need to pack," he said, ignoring my words. When I didn't instantly move, his voice grew loud and angry. "Get going!" He began packing his clothes and personal items into his suitcase by folding the dirty clothing into neat piles.

Craig had always been obsessive-compulsive, but I found this to be beyond the pale. "Are you seriously going to fold your dirty clothes to pack them away?"

"Of course I am, and you need to do the same," he responded harshly.

I laughed. "You're joking, right?"

"No Goddammit, now get your suitcase packed." He was losing his temper. "Or you're not going home with me!"

Wow. Tears filled my eyes. I had not been braced for this. I said, "I've got to run an errand. I'll meet you at checkout." I left the room, slamming the door hard behind me.

I found myself walking down to the wedding chapel to see the clerk and waited until she was alone. Once she was, I said hesitantly and softly, "Is it possible to annul our marriage?"

"Did you consummate it?" she asked firmly.

I hesitated because it wasn't like we hadn't already had sex before the marriage. "Well, yes," I said faintly.

"Then you'll have to go to Reno and get it done. You're married now in the eyes of the law. You can't just annul it. You'll have to get a divorce." She was adamant.

"Okay," I said weakly and left. I went to the room, threw my stuff into the suitcase, and dragged it to the lobby, where Craig was already in line to check out. I joined him.

"Where did you go?" he demanded.

"I went to see about getting an annulment. The clerk said we'd have to go to Reno," I replied flatly.

Craig didn't say anything. He just stared at me with a question on his face. I didn't speak. "Let's check out," he said finally.

We took a taxi to the airport and discovered our flight home had very few people on it, so Craig and I sat wherever we wanted. He chose a seat about midway back. Since we were married, I expected to sit together and maybe hold hands, but he wanted the extra space and told me to sit in front of him. It seemed like a longer flight going home than on the way there.

Had I done something really stupid in marrying this man I had sought out for two years? What kind of husband was he going to be if he was so distant and angry now? Had I honestly sealed my fate to this man? What was to become of me? My heart, mind, and stomach were all in knots.

When we got home, we went to my apartment. We'd only been there about twenty minutes when the phone rang. Rocky said, "Oh, hello? What's your last name?" he asked teasingly. I stammered as I told him. He laughed and said, "I thought so! I knew it!"

"We're just really tired," I said, still feeling the effects of all the alcohol in my system.

"I bet," he said jokingly. "You just rest, and we'll see you at work tomorrow." He hung up.

The next three weeks of rushed packing and storing items showed me that our married life was going to be stale and uneventful. I kept busy by packing up my personal items, including my many books, which would be stored. It was all about the business of moving and selling the property. There was no downtime in which we could enjoy each other as newlyweds.

"You don't have to control your thoughts.
You just have to stop letting them control you."
—Dan Millman

# Chapter 8

# Move to Germany

Craig and I began planning for the move to Germany. We decided to store his pickup truck and transport my newer model car. Since this was an unaccompanied tour for him (no government support for dependents), I thought we had to fly separately. I booked our flights, and his arrived in Frankfurt about forty minutes before mine did. When I finally got to the baggage claim area and located Craig, he was angry and said, "What took you so long? I was about to go on to my assignment without you."

I don't know if he intentionally played into my abandonment issues... but he had a razor-sharp way of provoking me and bringing my fears to the surface.

———— - ◇ - ————

Children rely completely on the adults in their lives to feel safe and cared for. When those adults (parents or caregivers) don't meet the child's emotional or physical needs, that child feels abandoned.

This kind of abandonment can leave a deep mark. A child who grows up without enough love, safety, or support can start to believe that the world isn't safe, that people can't be trusted, and that they don't deserve love or attention. They may even feel like something is wrong with them. Sometimes the abandonment is physical. That might look like:

- Being left alone or not properly watched
- Physical or sexual abuse

- Verbal or emotional abuse from a narcissistic parent
- Not being given enough food or proper meals
- Living without enough clothes, warmth, or stable housing

Other times, the abandonment is emotional. The child might have a roof over their head, but if their emotional needs are ignored, it's just as damaging. They may feel like they have to hide who they are. They start to believe things like:

- "It's not okay to make mistakes."
- "My needs don't matter."
- "I shouldn't show how I feel."

As these children grow up, many carry those early wounds into adulthood. They may struggle with the fear of being left again—especially in relationships. And even though fear of abandonment isn't a mental illness, it can still create a lot of anxiety and make it hard to form healthy connections. Abandonment in childhood can increase the risk of codependency, attachment anxiety, or ongoing low self-esteem. It can become a self-fulfilling pattern—because the more an insecure person acts clingy, needy, or controlling, the more likely they are to push others away.

I'll never forget one time when I was abandoned at six years old. I woke up in the back seat of a freezing cold, completely dark car. I soon realized I was all alone, and I was terrified. My parents had driven home from our regular Saturday trip into the city, got out, and proceeded to carry all the groceries into the house. The night was an inky black canvas, stretching endlessly around me as I sat alone in the car. This was very rural, and there were no streetlights. The world outside felt vast and unfathomable, a shadowy realm where unknown dangers lurked just beyond the car.

With each passing minute, a sense of dread coiled tighter in my stomach. I imagined monsters lurking just outside the window—phantoms of my own making, born from the shadows that danced across the lonely gravel road. My heart raced, pounding in my chest as I strained to listen for any sound, any sign that I was not forgotten.

Tears pooled in my eyes as I clutched my favorite stuffed animal, a floppy-ear, well-worn bear named Robert John. I whispered to him as if he could somehow shield me from the encroaching darkness. "They'll be right back," I assured Robert John.

In that moment, I learned what it felt like to be truly alone, feeling the weight of abandonment. The car, once a familiar fortress, transformed into a cage, its walls closing in around me. Scared, I got out in the pitch black of the night and ran into the family farmhouse. "Why didn't you wake me up when we got home?" I cried.

"We were going to come back out and get you," was the nonchalant reply I got as they continued to store away items that had been purchased. No one looked at me. No one saw my tears.

I felt utterly unimportant. This sense of abandonment stayed with me as it recurred throughout my childhood and teen years. At 16, my parents did something even worse that overwhelmed me with feelings of being insignificant.

During the summer of my junior year, I went to Lander, Wyoming, to participate in a work-study program. I returned home in August, excited to rejoin my friends as we started our much-anticipated senior year of high school.

When my sister Josie picked me up at the airport, she said, "Well, I've got some news for you." She hesitated while looking at me for some sort of reaction.

I had no idea she was about to reveal something that would completely change my life. "What is it?"

"Well, Mom and Dad moved from the cute little house in the city to a big rural farmhouse about twenty miles away." Again, I felt abandoned because I was not important enough to even be told about the move. My happy feelings of coming home disappeared. I felt like the rug was pulled out from under me, leaving me off-balance and confused. And, in that irrational way that children feel responsible when they shouldn't, I felt shame. Even though it was just my sister witnessing my shock and disappointment, it made it feel so real that "everyone else knew." Did my parents forget I existed, or what?

The new house was in a different school district, which meant I would not graduate with my peers. My clothes and personal items had been packed up and moved without my knowledge or consent. It took some getting used to a new place and school, but I made the best of it. I signed up for the new school's work-study program, which allowed me to attend classes in the morning and work in the city every afternoon, learning and practicing clerical skills. I was fortunate to cope with my "nice, normal family" by having goals and staying busy in pursuit of them.

———— ◇ ————

Once in Germany, in the early fall of 1986, when it was just turning cold, we went to Bad Kreuznach where Craig was assigned to work. We began searching for a place to live, which turned out to be somewhat of a challenge.

One arrangement option was to live in a home with Germans. We'd have our own small bedroom, share a bathroom with the family, and have access to their kitchen. I was not keen on this, but Craig seemed to think it was a good idea. I believe he thought he could keep closer tabs on me with that setup. The people we would be living with could advise him where I was and what I was doing. I was also not comfortable with the lack of privacy we would have.

We finally discovered a high-rise a few miles from the Army Kaserne and rented a fourth-floor apartment. It was a quaint one-bedroom, but it afforded the privacy I thought we needed as newlyweds.

Craig's work began immediately. I looked for a job and learned that the Commanding General of the Army division to which Craig was assigned was looking for a personal assistant. I applied for the position and was accepted. It was an honor to serve in such a capacity as the Executive Secretary for a Major General and his wife. I worked directly for him, with guidance from the aide-de-camp.

Once we were both gainfully employed, I reviewed my academic accomplishments, which were meager compared to what I had hoped to have achieved by then. I had been quietly taking correspondence courses from various colleges and universities across the United States in anticipation of getting a Bachelor's Degree in Business Administration from Columbia College, Columbia, Missouri.

I began adding experiential learning credits and acquired many business and behavioral science credits by passing the available tests. When I became familiar with the military Kaserne, I learned that continuing education was not only readily available but also sought after and widely accepted by both the military and civilians. That was the reverse of what I had heard from Craig, who said, "We don't need any more enlightenment." Perhaps he spoke for himself.

Once in Germany, because the military was so keen on educational advancement, I was able to start taking multiple college and university extension program courses. I started earning a degree in Business Administration, but after completing all the required courses, I began taking electives in Psychology.

I actually felt like my life was more on track and enjoyable there in Germany than it had been in the States. I woke up each day with something to look forward to.

> "The strongest people are those
> who win battles we know nothing about."
> —Unknown

# Chapter 9

# The Accident

Who could imagine we'd become stage actors? In 1986, the evening after Christmas of our first year in Germany, when Nixon was President and *The Color Purple* was on the big screen, I was reading at home in our cozy apartment and munching on *Gebrannte Mandeln*, German-style holiday nuts. After a few months in Germany, Craig and I had begun participating in the Kaserne's community theater. We had just finished performing in *On Golden Pond*, and Craig was at rehearsal that evening, preparing for a new show.

My sister Josie called, and I answered in a chipper voice, feeling positive and in a holiday mood. "Hi! Did you have a good Christmas?"

She said, "There's been an accident." She paused for me to react.

I immediately sobered. My heart was in my throat. "What happened?"

She began slowly, tearfully, "Mom and Dad were in an automobile accident when Dad was on his way to a doctor appointment. Their van skidded on black ice. Dad was killed. Mom is in the hospital in critical condition," she sobbed.

"Oh my God." Tears sprang to my eyes. It was too much to take in. "How bad is Mom's condition?" Not only was I concerned about her degree of injury, I was immediately worried about Mom's livelihood now that Dad was gone.

"Well, she is in a coma and has been seriously injured," Josie said.

"How bad? Is she going to live?"

"We don't know yet. Can you come home?"

My heart skipped a beat. "Of course. I'll have to let you know about when," I said. "I love you," I added.

"I love you, too," she said before hanging up the phone.

My world shattered in an instant with that phone call. The news struck me like lightning—sharp, sudden, and utterly devastating. I felt an overwhelming sense of disbelief; I'd been transported into a nightmare from which I couldn't awaken.

The gravity of the situation weighed heavily on my chest, making it hard to breathe. I felt a mix of shock and confusion, grappling with the reality that my father was gone. A profound emptiness enveloped me, and I struggled to comprehend a life without him. Memories flooded my mind, but they brought an acute sense of loss instead of comfort.

---

Dad started out as a farmer. Then he went into the insurance business, and I was his secretary because I could type and do his office work. In the 1960s, farming was difficult. When I was in junior high school, we moved to Grand Junction, Colorado, because Dad had once gone through there on a troop train and decided that he wanted to live there one day. The location's natural beauty, community spirit, and the promise of a new beginning called to him. Dad was an avid outdoorsman, as was I, and he went fishing or hunting nearly every weekend with Mom and usually me. Being quite a tomboy, I was always outside, either playing in the barn or pig pen, or following Dad as he worked around the farm.

He was in his sixties when he died. He already suffered from back and joint pain and was being treated for hemochromatosis (dangerous iron levels), which was where he was going when the accident occurred. He always said, "I want to die with my boots on." And he did.

---

As I processed the news about my mother lying in a hospital bed, fighting for her life, my heart sank deeper into despair. I felt a surge of helplessness; I was thousands of miles away, unable to be by her side or offer support. Anxiety gnawed at me as I wondered about her condition and the uncertainty of her future.

Anger simmered beneath the surface—anger at the circumstances, at the cruel randomness of fate, and the world for continuing to spin while my life had come to a standstill. I grappled with guilt, too, questioning if I could have done something to prevent this tragedy or if I could have done or said something different before it happened.

In the hours that followed, I found myself caught in a whirlwind of emotions—grief, sorrow, and an aching longing for the past. All sense of holiday warmth and joy had become a disturbing slap in the face. All of life seemed hollow and distant.

I called the community theater, but I was so overwrought with emotion that I couldn't even explain what had happened. Craig only understood something was terribly wrong, and he came home immediately, though it seemed like forever before he walked through the door.

While I was waiting for him, I managed to call the General's aide-de-camp and tell him what had happened and that I needed some time off.

He said, "The American Red Cross must be notified so you and your husband can fly home." He hung up.

Then, the Major General called me personally shortly thereafter, informing me, "You don't have to wait for Red Cross notification—just go, and I'm sorry for your loss."

Craig was upset about the news and just quietly supported me in making arrangements for us to return to the States. He was planning to go with me, which I appreciated.

---

What happened between hearing the go-ahead to leave and getting to my mom will forever be a blur. Craig and I were told to go to an air base to catch a flight to the East Coast, but when we arrived, we were advised that the plane had been grounded and we would need to drive to a different location. Craig was as frustrated as I was, but he didn't let it bother him and took the setbacks in stride. I was pleased that he didn't become upset or aggravated with the confusion and take it out on me, which was behavior I had learned to expect.

We eventually arrived at Ronald Reagan Washington International Airport in Arlington, Virginia, and had to find and book flights to Grand Junction, Colorado, where my mother was hospitalized. It was several more grueling hours before we finally landed in Colorado.

Each passing moment felt like an eternity, amplifying my helplessness and despair. The flights felt excruciatingly long, each a painful reminder of the miles that separated me from my family. My mind was a tempest of anxiety, imagining every possible scenario, replaying endless, random memories, and yearning for the comfort of my parents' presence. My heart stopped mid-beat when I remembered I no longer had two parents…my dad was gone forever.

Craig was exceptionally quiet and complacent. His emotional support was helpful, but I felt a growing frustration and impatience. The mundane rituals of travel—checking in, waiting at gates, enduring layovers—were agonizing reminders of the urgency of my situation. I longed to be there, to hold my mother's hand, to grieve with my sisters, and to face this crisis together. Instead, I felt trapped in limbo, my heart aching for home while my body remained suspended in transit.

The landscape below changed with each flight, but I felt disconnected from the world outside. The beauty and lights of the cities felt irrelevant against the backdrop of my internal turmoil. I had been staying in touch by telephone from various points on our journey for any updates on my mother's condition, talking with either Sarah or Josie. No change.

*"Trauma is like a storm that disrupts our lives;*
*recovery is the rainbow that appears when we learn to embrace our scars."*
—Unknown

# Chapter 10

# Home Again

*What if she doesn't wake up? Who will tell her Dad is dead? What am I going to do?*

My thoughts tormented me, relentless needles against my already aching heart. I was relieved to be on a plane that would get me to my mother as fast as possible, but it seemed to take an eternity. When we finally landed in Grand Junction, I felt I had not only crossed over an ocean and then state after state, but had been skirting the edge of an emotional chasm the entire trip. The exhaustion of travel weighed heavily on me, but it paled compared to the emotional burden I carried. The relief of being back home overshadowed by the reality of what awaited me—a heart-wrenching journey through grief and uncertainty.

Craig and I landed and got off the plane. I walked through the airport in a daze, then heard Craig call out, "Hello!" My three sisters were there, as was Ralph.

After we all hugged, I asked, "Any news?"

"Nothing," said Sarah. She had been the RN on duty when my mother was transported to the Emergency Room by helicopter that fateful night. "She was combative, which isn't a good sign." She hesitated, then added, "They performed surgery removing her spleen and stitched up wounds. She is in a coma." We were all bewildered and grieving. No one asked us about our long trip from another continent. No one talked about their children. No one had energy for the usual pleasantries of a family reunion.

The world outside continued on, but I felt trapped in a moment of profound loss, grappling with the fragility of life and the deep love for my family.

Craig made himself scarce but was available if I needed to lean on him. I didn't. Then he learned that his ex and son were also in Colorado, so he arranged to spend time with them. I don't know if their being in Colorado was coincidental or not, but I was happy that he had an outlet and a place to be, so I could focus on family issues. Maybe he called her on a pay phone during our layover…I didn't have the energy to give it much thought.

Just before we entered Mom's room, Sarah advised me again, "She looks pretty bad. She is bruised all over, and if you want to see her first and then leave the room, we would understand it completely."

I agreed, and the four of us went into her room together. I didn't recognize her swollen and battered face. The earring in her left-pierced ear had been ripped out because her ear lobe was no longer intact, and her left eye was seriously damaged and appeared beyond repair. She was lying on her back, although I knew the nursing staff would routinely reposition her.

As I stood by her bedside, I felt a profound sorrow wash over me. The sight of her injuries was almost too much to bear. It felt surreal as if witnessing a cruel distortion of reality. I longed to reach out to hold her hand and tell her everything would be alright, but instead, I was met with the hard truth of her condition. The comatose stillness felt like a void, amplifying my feelings of helplessness and despair.

I grappled with a deep sense of fear. *What if she didn't wake up?* The thought was a dark cloud looming over my heart. I yearned for the warmth of her smile, her laughter, and the comfort of her embrace. In the silence of the hospital room, I felt an aching emptiness, a longing for the connection that seemed just out of reach. I suddenly knew what utter helplessness felt like; I couldn't help her, and she couldn't help me, and we were both in a bad way.

I whispered words of love and encouragement, hoping she could hear me and feel my presence. Amidst the pain, I also felt a flicker of hope. I held on to the memory of her strength and resilience throughout my life, believing that she was still there, fighting to come back to us.

I didn't want to leave the room. I didn't even want to take my eyes off of her. The sight of her, despite the disastrous look of her face, reminded me of the bond we shared. It was a reminder of the love that transcends even the most difficult circumstances. In my heart, I clung to the hope that the woman I remembered—the caring mother, the guiding light—was still inside, waiting for the moment to return to us.

"What time will the doctor be here?" I asked quietly.

"They make rounds at about seven in the morning," Sarah said. It was then 10:00 p.m.

"I want to see the doctor when he comes in," I said. "I want to know her prognosis." We positioned two chairs, one on either side of my mother. Her four daughters (Sarah, Josie, Rene, and I) sat two at a time, taking shifts, holding her hand, talking to her and each other, and including her in the conversation.

"Hey, Mom," I said, "I flew all the way from Europe just to see you, and here you are asleep. What's up with that?"

Josie added, "Yeah, we know you're faking it just to get attention." Mom did not respond. We continued this vigil throughout the first night, watching her as she slept and looking for any signs of recognition or awareness. There were none.

The next morning, two doctors arrived: an older one who seemed to be in charge and a younger man who stayed quiet but closely observed. The older one said, "She's a tough old bird because she is still alive." Mom was in her mid-sixties and had experienced a variety of physical problems over the years, including walking around for a week with a burst appendix, surviving breast cancer, and a broken leg. "I can't give you any guidance about the case except that the next 48 hours will be critical—if she makes it that far." I felt my heart in my throat when I heard "IF she makes it…"

He was calm and professional. He spoke candidly and with authority. "People in comas routinely never regain consciousness, and if they do, there is often brain damage associated with their recovery." The doctor touched Mom's hand and asked her if she could feel that. Mom gave no response. We were all shaken by the doctor's lack of even one encouraging word, and it settled in for me that her chances weren't good.

Josie and I went to the cafeteria for a break shortly after the doctors left. Ralph followed us and offered, "I saw a beautiful funeral spray for sale in the gift shop with lots of pretty flowers."

We both stared at him, incredulous. We silently turned our backs to him and ordered from the cafeteria line. He shrugged as if he didn't understand why that upset us.

Later that day, when I was alone with Sarah, I asked, "Where is Dad?"

She replied bluntly, "Oh, he's already been cremated."

I was dumbfounded that it had happened so soon and that he was just gone. I had expected to be able to view his body or have one last moment with him, rather than nothing. I broke down and cried. I was again left out of another important family decision and process. Josie consoled me, "I can't believe she just told you like that," she paused. "Are you okay?"

---

Did no one even consider that my dad and I would care to say goodbye to one another, one last time? It felt as though a crucial piece of my father's journey had been taken from me, and I was left standing on the sidelines, grappling with the weight of my own helplessness. How could such a monumental event have happened without my knowledge? At that moment, I felt a sharp pang of hurt, a visceral ache that cut deep. Learning, like it was an afterthought, that important and truly final decisions had been made without my input or even a simple notification felt like an erasure of my place in the family story. My connection to my father had been invalidated by my "nice, normal family." I had envisioned being part of the process of honoring him in some way, but instead, I felt excluded.

It was not just the absence of my father that left me feeling lost; it was the realization that I had been overlooked and left out from a moment so significant, one that deserved to be shared. I felt like an invisible ghost in my own family, drifting through a painful reality where I was not only mourning my father but also the bonds that seemed to be slipping away. I felt overwhelmed with everything from sadness, disbelief, shame, hurt, anger, and loneliness, on top of a mountain of grief.

In the aftermath of that revelation, I wanted to lash out, to demand answers and acknowledgment, yet I also felt an overwhelming sense of vulnerability. The loss of my father was compounded by the loss of my voice in the very decisions that honored his life. It was a painful reminder of how grief can fracture connections, leaving us grappling with our emotions in solitude.

After our break, Josie and I went back to the ICU room. Luckily, the hospital staff allowed us in there at all times. At night, we stayed at the house of a relative of Josie's, near the hospital.

Two weeks later, Craig was still away visiting his ex and their seven-year-old son. I had no idea if their stay in Colorado was pre-planned or Craig's idea as a result of my parents' accident, and I didn't care.

I went to bed early one evening, and as I started to doze off, my father appeared to me. He was wearing a plaid shirt, as usual, but he was standing up straight, apparently in no pain like he had been in when he was alive. He said to me, "You girls have to work together now and help Mom." I was eager to talk to him, and just as I began to respond, he disappeared as he floated up into the corner of the bedroom. I was initially afraid to tell my sisters because I thought they would laugh or think I was crazy.

Two days later, I confessed to Josie what had happened. I was surprised when she became slightly indignant and said, "Why didn't he come to me?" We had heard of such things happening a few days after a person passed.

At the hospital, we continued to hold Mom's hand, rub her arm, and talk to her as if she were present and responding. We did this for twenty-five days, with the doctor coming in daily, touching her and talking to her with no reaction, and just negatively shaking his head, saying, "No purposeful response."

We disagreed with that impression, and I said, "We can feel her hand tighten." He looked at me and quickly strangled my infinitesimal hope.

"It's common, and you shouldn't be encouraged by that."

*"The pain you feel today is the strength you feel tomorrow."*
—Unknown

# Chapter 11

# Turtle Soup

Day 26. When Mom was finally helped up by the nurses and put into a chair beside her hospital bed, I thought her face felt warm, so I wet a cloth with cool water and placed it on her forehead. At first, there was no reaction. Then she reached up and pulled it off her face. Sarah and I were stunned. That was the first deliberate action she had taken since the accident. The staff took notice and returned her to the bed. I believe the doctor was notified.

The doctor came in shortly after. He said, "I understand you've seen some changes." He walked to my mother's bedside and put his hand on hers. She did not react. "Well, it's been a while since she's been in a coma. The next few days, with increased physical therapy, will be telling."

We started talking to her more. Her eyes were open but stationary. She said nothing, but when we asked her to blink if she could hear us, she did. We squeezed her hand, and she squeezed back. She was moved from the ICU to a regular room, where she received more intensive daily physical therapy.

The television was on constantly, and she seemed to be watching it, but we weren't sure because of her silence and lack of responsiveness. Because she loved butterflies, we got a cloth butterfly at the gift shop and hung it above her bed. It went with her each time she was moved from one room or facility to another.

Two days later, the physical therapist was working with Mom at her bedside. The television was airing a game show. I said, "Are you feeling spunky today?"

She ignored me as usual, and then she said very clearly, "Turtle soup."

"What are you talking about?" I asked her. Then I heard the TV game show contestant say, "Turtle soup." She had always watched game shows and was good at answering the questions. "You got it, Mom," I said, smiling through my tears.

We hadn't realized she was that cognizant because she had been so quiet. Mom slowly began to acknowledge us girls, and she seemed to recognize who we were. She started talking a little more every day. She had no memory of the accident, and she didn't seem to know we'd been talking to her for the past month.

The doctor said, "We know there is brain damage, but not to what extent. She will have to learn to crawl and walk again. Don't expect her to return to the level of functioning she was before the accident."

Unfortunately, her left eye was severely damaged, which made it impossible for her to read, one of her favorite pastimes. Another was working on crossword puzzles, which she continued to do masterfully.

She was transferred to a well-known rehabilitation center in town and started daily physical, speech, and occupational therapies. They conducted water therapy, but she hated it and screamed whenever they lowered her into the water.

Even though it was wintertime, Josie and I went out to get Mom an ice cream. We returned to find her sitting in the day room of the facility with an empty chair pulled up next to her, almost touching her wheelchair. We were surprised, and I asked, "Did someone come to visit you?"

She said firmly, "It was your Daddy."

We looked at each other and didn't know what to say. We gave her the ice cream. She never spoke of it again.

After about thirty days of our bereavement leave in the United States, I was apprehensive about making plans to return to Germany. Because Mom was improving, Craig and I knew we'd have to go back to Germany soon and started making those arrangements. He had spent most of the time with his ex and son, for which he was appreciative, and I was pleased he had the opportunity to do so. It helped me be less concerned about him so I could focus my attention on Mom.

Josie still lived in the area, as did Alice. Sarah worked at the hospital where Mom was admitted. I was the only one who had to leave. It was difficult because I knew I wouldn't be back for at least another year. But I knew Mom was in good hands with Sarah being an RN and Josie being an LPN. I was still concerned about how she would get along.

I remained determined to earn my college degree. I said to Craig, "Maybe I should stay here and go full-time to Mesa College." Colorado Mesa University was located near the rehabilitation center, and I couldn't help but long to complete my degree.

"You would do that? Let me go back to Germany by myself so you could go to school?" He was not happy about me even suggesting such a thing. So, I let the idea go.

There was a memorial service for my father, which was well attended by people from the community. It at least provided some closure for me. I was not involved in setting up that service, but whoever did it clearly felt strongly about my father and his legacy. I at least left feeling good about his life.

— ◇ —

We flew back to Bad Kreuznach via Frankfurt. It was 1986, and the charity song "We Are the World" by the supergroup USA for Africa topped the charts. Phil Collins won Album of the Year for "No Jacket Required," and Bon Jovi's "Slippery When Wet" became one of the best-selling albums of all time. World news was often the topic of conversation among us on the base. There was the Chernobyl disaster, the overthrow of Ferdinand Marcos in the Philippines, and Mikhail Gorbachev introducing Glasnost and Perestroika in the Soviet Union. And one time, in late January of that year, there was news that I will never forget hearing, as it felt so personal.

I was at my desk in the General's office and was asked to make a long-distance call, which required the assistance of a switchboard operator. When I reached the operator, she was crying very hard and said, "I am so sorry!"

Not having been informed, I said, "What is it?"

"The Challenger…the Challenger blew up on takeoff," she said, her voice heavy with a German accent.

"Oh my God," was all I could get out at that moment. I told her I'd call back a little later. It was devastating news that rocked the world, particularly the Americans serving overseas. It somehow made us feel isolated from the situation and helpless to do anything about it. Our distance from the horror didn't make it less crushing; we were Americans, and it seemed like a personal tragedy.

On April 26, we were scheduled to travel to Russia, specifically to the town of Kyiv (now in Ukraine); however, we were not allowed to go due to Craig's military status. As a member of the US Armed Forces, Russia would not grant him a visa, so we decided to forgo that particular trip. Considering what happened that day, we were thankful we couldn't go because the Chornobyl Nuclear Plant exploded.

We did get to visit many different countries during that second year we were in Germany. We went to Amsterdam, England, Belgium, Luxembourg, the French countryside, and Paris as well as Malta. We also visited my cousins in Sweden.

In May, after Mom was discharged from rehabilitation, she moved in with Sarah and Ralph. In all the locations Craig and I visited I found souvenirs to send to her as she continued her recovery at Sarah's house. I sent her crystal butterflies from everywhere. At one point, I found a kit that I sent to her so she could watch the chrysalis turn into a butterfly. I sent her sweatshirts from every town we visited. I wrote her letters that my sister read to her. A couple of times, I typed her notes in extra-large letters so she could read them.

In June of 1986, nearing the end of our time in Germany, I was pleased to have completed all the course requirements for both my Business Administration and Psychology Degrees, and I was awarded a Dual Degree. Craig was excited about finally being able to retire after twenty years in uniform.

He said, "I want to live in Tennessee, where I was born."

I asked, "Are there any lakes we could live on to be on the water and maybe buy a pontoon boat?"

"We'll have to see," he said.

"The individual has always had to struggle to keep from being overwhelmed by the tribe.
If you try it, you will be lonely often, and sometimes frightened.
But no price is too high to pay for the privilege of owning yourself."
—RUDYARD KIPLING

## CHAPTER 12

# MOVE BACK TO THE U.S.

"No, you're not getting a cat."

Craig didn't even ask why I wanted a cat. I had decided that a cuddly companion would be good company, help me to feel less lonely, and give me respite from the tension so prevalent in the household. Thank goodness I still had a trace of self-esteem left, just enough to go against Craig's unreasonable stance of forbidding me to get a rescue cat.

It was September of 1986, and Craig and I had just returned to the United States. After visiting Mom in her senior apartment in Salt Lake City, we moved to Morristown, Tennessee, where we discovered Cherokee Lake, also known as Cherokee Reservoir. We found a three-bedroom house on the lake with a basement. A large wooden deck ran the length of the house on the lake side, where we sat and had coffee each morning. We purchased a pontoon boat and spent hours on the lake fishing and swimming. Or rather, I swam off the boat and Craig fished off another side of the boat. We generally didn't do activities together.

Since I (finally) had my college degree, I applied for project management positions—and was informed by the good ole' boy Tennessee network that, as a woman, I had to be hired as secretarial staff and then promoted at the discretion of the company.

This did not sit well with me, so I applied for Army Reserve positions around the country; there. I was respected as a capable person who had earned the rank of Sergeant First Class, E-7, and was paid accordingly.

I started in October of 1986, with winter in full force, by working with the security team for the Annual General Conference, always held for two weeks in St. Louis. Each year, a group of the same military reservists convened in St. Louis to provide security for those attending the conference. We were housed at the host hotel for the duration of the conference.

The security staff members were attached to the US Army Personnel Center's Security Office and worked partially out of that location, setting up prior to the conference. I worked in both locations, along with the security detail, providing clerical support wherever needed. I really enjoyed my active military status and the camaraderie it afforded me. I was considered "one of the guys." They appreciated my work so much that I was invited back for the next three years. Craig was not happy with these frequent periods of me being away from home, but I gained so much respect and admiration during my time on active duty that it only drew me in more. I firmly believe that having this one oasis, this one place where I could be myself—even my smart, highly-trained, assertive, outgoing self—kept me sane like a cool drink of water means you won't die of thirst.

When I returned home to Tennessee from a military assignment in November of 1986, I signed up at a temporary agency to do secretarial work, but made sure the agency knew I was not looking for anything permanent. I had no plan to completely give up future Reservist opportunities.

I began working at a mental health clinic where therapists were in abundance, so I decided to do some psychotherapy work myself. I had been in numerous situations before where I talked with therapists who were generally in training. This time, I decided to talk with one PhD level psychotherapist. After we met, he immediately decided I wanted out of the relationship which I actually felt was a little premature. He also accused me of moving from one relationship to another only to learn that the new man in my life developed "clay feet" and then I was ready to move on. I denied this scenario and he eventually diagnosed me with Major Depressive Disorder and administered Prozac. This seemed to help more than I could have imagined. We discussed my relationships with men, beginning with my brother-in-law and how that related to my interactions with men throughout my life. He conducted interpersonal psychodynamic therapy. That style of treatment really helped me understand a lot about how my relationships with others were affected, particularly with men. The therapist said, "Do you realize how you relate to others affects how your personality comes across, and they, in turn, relate to you?" Over time, it became apparent to me that the two men I had chosen to become involved with were both controlling narcissistic misogynists.

"Do you recognize that pattern of behavior in anyone from your life as you were growing up?" my therapist asked

*How could I not see that?* I wondered.

I began to piece things together. My brother-in-law was the most present male role model in my life when I was growing up. My father generally worked two jobs and wasn't home much during my adolescent years. But Ralph was present a good portion of the time, and he had a definite effect on my feelings and my understanding of what men were about.

Whenever I heard or read news articles about childhood sexual abuse, I felt sorry for the victims. I said to my therapist, "You mean every family doesn't have an oversexed uncle or brother-in-law in it?"

At the age of twenty-eight, it became clear to me that I was a statistic. I finally learned I had been sexually abused as a child. For me, my "nice, normal family" included adults being negligent, careless, and abusive—all things I was blind to as a child.

Refer to "Blind Spots" in Appendix A.

—◇—

In 1988, after returning from Germany, Craig's controlling behavior became more apparent. The reason he didn't want me to work was to keep me what the Tennessee menfolk referred to as "dumb, barefoot, and pregnant," which would preclude me from going anywhere, learning anything, or exercising independent thought.

During that summer, a neighbor said to us, "I saw a History Channel documentary on the Civil War that was very educational."

I responded with sarcasm, "Oh gosh, we don't need any more education," parroting my husband.

Craig intervened, "Well, of course we do! Education is extremely important." I just glared at him and walked away from both men.

I felt lonely and alone, so I said, "I want to get a cat."

"You don't need a cat, for goodness sake," Craig said.

"But I was thinking that a rescue cat …"

He cut me off with, "No, you're not getting a cat."

Despite his additional derogatory remarks, I found a white cat with blue eyes at the feline rescue mission. I learned it had been adopted before, then returned after a couple of weeks. I obtained the phone number of the individual who had adopted it and called to determine if it was aggressive or destructive.

The woman first said, "No, we got a new baby in the home and didn't want the cat near the baby." I asked if the cat had been disruptive in any way because I didn't want to adopt a problem animal. The woman then reluctantly said, "The cat is deaf. He can't hear anything."

Based on that information alone, I wanted to adopt him. I did, and because he was fluffy and white, I named him "Q-Tip." Yes, he definitely was deaf, but we got along just fine. He was an indoor cat, but as a treat, I would take him out onto the deck and sit with him on my lap, which he enjoyed. He seemed very happy, and his contentment was contagious, just as I had hoped.

I discovered an unusual situation regarding my feelings during this three-year period of my life from 1986 to 1989. I looked forward to weekdays when I could go to work, but I hated the weekends because they were so uncomfortable being around Craig.

— ◇ —

I found more opportunities for active duty in the US Army Reserve. I worked 30 days at Tooele Army Depot, Utah, during one summer, then went back for another two weeks. I was able to attend the Noncommissioned Officers (NCO) Academy and was promoted to Sergeant First Class, E-7. I attended an Instructor's Academy and was awarded the identifier on my Military Occupational Specialty (MOS) as an instructor. I continued to serve in an administrative role for the Annual General Conference.

During one of my temporary duty periods, I had a telephone conversation with Craig. He said, "I'm going to close Q-Tip up in that workspace he'd found to hide in." I suddenly felt guilty for leaving my cat in Craig's care—I knew he would not treat him as well as I had.

Craig said, "You shouldn't go off and leave him. He gets scruffy-looking and doesn't take care of himself when you're gone. He sits in the window and pouts." I wondered if this was actually a projection on Craig's part about himself. He never got used to me being gone and leaving him to fend for himself.

In early 1989, I was away and learned that I couldn't reach Craig in the evenings by phone because he was "at the VFW club." Shortly after that, he got a job working there. When I returned home for a short leave, a woman called him at the house, nearly every day. He said it was just someone from work (at the VFW). I suspected he was having an affair, but I didn't confront him. I, too, was having sexual liaisons with the soldiers with whom I was on temporary duty.

"If having a soul means being able to feel
love and loyalty and gratitude,
then animals are better off than a lot of humans."
—James Herriot

## Chapter 13

# Warrant Officer Academy

In May of 1989, I applied for and was selected to attend the US Army Warrant Officer Academy at Fort McCoy, Wisconsin. Craig, a retired Master Sergeant, remained notably silent about my plans. The unspoken tension of my potentially outranking him hung in the air, though we never discussed it.

My November arrival in Sparta, Wisconsin, set the tone for what was to come. Standing at the small rural airport on Sunday, the day before training began, I discovered that my duffel bag had not made the journey with me. The chill in the air bit through my civilian clothes as I made my way to Fort McCoy to report my situation to the post authorities, who merely said, "We'll take it under advisement."

On Monday, the first day of class, I stood out in my dark jeans and turtle-neck shirt among a sea of battle-dress uniforms. As one of only three women in a class of forty-five, I already felt conspicuous. Then the Commander singled me out, stating, "We expect everyone to be in uniform," which only amplified my discomfort. We were told, "You'll be weighed and measured, and if you exceed the weight limit for your height, you will be sent home."

During the weigh-in, three staff members who were to determine accurate weight and height decided I was two inches shorter than my documented height, so they could classify me as "overweight."

The two women and one man measured my chest and hips with a tape measure. Their hands-on measurements of my body left me feeling totally violated and powerless. One officer said, "Oh, you're too fat. You'll never pass the PT Test, and then you'll be sent home."

A Physical Training (PT) test in the military is an assessment of physical fitness to evaluate a service member's ability to perform their duties. It's really hard, by design. Despite their predictions of failure, I excelled in the PT test, completing the required push-ups, sit-ups, and a two-mile run with time left over to encourage my peers to accomplish their run within the time allowed. That did not go unnoticed.

The training staff's authority was immediately apparent. During our first bathroom break, we found the entire cadre, including the Commanding Officer, waiting in the hallway. We snapped to attention, holding that position until dismissed.

When we were back in the meeting room, the Commander said, "We expect everyone to be in uniform, with gleaming boots. There will be mandatory morning runs at the pace of the fastest man in the company. Anyone who falls out will be examined in the field with an anal thermometer. This is for anyone who can't keep up the pace." He continued, "You will puke up your breakfast because of the intensity of the running we will participate in."

In our Public Speaking Class, we were told, "You'll receive a piece of paper with a topic of discussion on it. You'll have one minute to prepare, and then you must present your assigned topic by speaking to the class for 15 minutes." When my turn came, I was given a slip of paper with no writing on it. I spoke on the pulp and paper industry, for which I received applause from peers and staff.

At the end of the second day, Tuesday, my duffel bag had arrived and been dumped upside down onto the floor of my assigned room—one at the end of the open bay area where 45 men were housed and slept. There was an open-door policy. My room door was not to be closed.

I not only found my duffel bag contents in a pile my whole quarters had been ransacked. My underwear was stuck to the window screen, and my bed was upended, standing sideways against the wall. All of my clothes and personal items were strewn across the floor of the room. With thirty minutes to lights out, there was only enough time to set up my clothes for the next day, reassemble my bed, and get in it. I tried to sleep while keeping a watchful eye on the doorway, where my male classmates were just a few feet away.

Wednesday was filled with more physical exercise and classes. At the end of the day, my room and the open bay had been ransacked again, with clothing thrown on the floor and foot lockers turned over. We had no time to organize our clothing or set up our closets according to regulations. It was time for lights out again. However, since all of the other attendees had their luggage from the beginning, their items were already established in a good place, so it took little time and effort for them to correct their problems.

I realized then, my third sleepless night, that I would not be able to catch up or put my clothes in the proper space in the closet, with my clothes and personal items all strewn around the room. The frustration of knowing I was there to do my best and follow the rules, yet literally being prevented from doing so, was overwhelming. So, Thursday morning, I approached the Commander and said, "Sir, I want to leave the Academy."

All he said was, "No," and walked away. I then approached each of the members of the cadre individually and told them I wanted to leave. They informed me that only the Commander had that authority. I continued to go through the classes and participated as expected.

On Friday, I approached the Commander again. "Sir, I want to leave the Academy." He said, "No," and walked away again.

Before he was out of sight, I said, "I want to speak to the Chaplain." My recruiter had advised me of this option in case I ever found myself in a situation where I wasn't being heard, since requesting time with the Chaplain could not be denied.

The Commander slowed down when he heard that, then ignored me and walked away again. Another day went by with still no time or opportunity to catch up on getting my room in order.

Military discipline is good because it creates efficiency through order, coordination, and decisive action, which is vital for mission success and saving lives. It helps to instill traits like self-control, accountability, and resilience, leading to personal growth and improved performance in other areas of life. At the time, I didn't have the words to clearly point out that I was not resisting any rules or chain of command, only complaining that I was being targeted because of my gender, period.

I continued to participate in the various drills, ceremonies, and classes presented despite feeling extremely depressed and exceptionally anxious about my ongoing and unaddressed situation.

Finally, on Friday afternoon, I was told to meet the Chaplain in the Conference Room. When we met, I explained about the ongoing sexually-oriented harassment and how it triggered memories of my past trauma. The Chaplain cut the meeting short because he was uncomfortable with the state of my emotional upset.

Later that day, at dinner, I overheard my classmates discussing how the Commander had called my husband about my desire to leave and that Craig's response had been, "Well, I don't know." They were astounded that my husband did not stick up for me. The next day, I was told I could pick up my ticket at the office and go home. I collected the items from my room and repacked my duffel bag.

When I returned home at the end of the week, my husband's only comment about the entire ordeal was to confirm that what I had overheard was accurate. When the Commander called him and told him I wanted to leave, he said, "I don't know what to tell you." His words spoke volumes about the complex dynamics of power, gender, and marriage in military life, leaving me to navigate the aftermath of this disturbing experience alone, with only my therapist to address it.

I lost a lot of respect for my husband following that ordeal, and I began mentally packing, with leaving him in mind.

What I learned from this experience was that I should not have gone to a military academy unprepared. Some alternatives I could have pursued were to seek support from my peers to help me get my closet and room in order, or to ask the Commander for extra time to establish myself correctly, but I doubted either was a viable option. What I learned about my husband was that he didn't have my back, and I could not depend on him to protect me or my interests. It left me feeling bitter and uncared for and reminded me of the abandonment I felt when left alone in the car at age six.

> "Be miserable. Or motivate yourself. Whatever
> has to be done, it's always your choice."
> —WAYNE DYER

## CHAPTER 14

# AN UNPLANNED STAY IN CAPE COD

The scent of sea air filled my nostrils the moment I stepped out of my car at Camp Edwards for my three-month tour of duty. It was early summer, and the weather was lovely. I surveyed my new surroundings. Yes, this was exactly what I needed.

In the early spring of 1990, I had submitted my application to become a Parole Officer in Tennessee, where I was still living with Craig. Nothing panned out.

I contacted my military personnel office and asked if there were any short active-duty tours available. The answer was "Nova Scotia" and "Camp Edwards." I said, "I'll pass."

After two more calls over the period of a month, I called again and learned there was no change. I said, "Where is Camp Edwards, anyway?"

I heard the rustling of paper, which I envisioned was a map being pulled open. "Cape Cod."

I said, "Oh, yes, I'll take that."

When I told Craig, he said, "Just don't come back." I continued to talk about the assignment, and he said, "Did you hear what I said?"

"Yes, I heard you," I replied.

Orders were cut, and I drove to Massachusetts. My second soon-to-be ex-husband's parting words, "Don't come back," crept into my serenity. It had been a huge mistake eloping to Vegas with a guy I'd met on Temporary Duty (TDY). I left a prized position as a Personnel Senior Sergeant to marry that loser. Yet that was just one of my many regrets for trusting that cheating, controlling jerk.

To say I had kissed enough frogs to last a lifetime was an understatement, but I was free again and planned to make the most of my time in Cape Cod. Technically, I wasn't divorced yet, but I knew with certainty that it was over. As soon as this TDY was over, I'd handle the formalities.

"Hello," I said, smiling at the civilian behind the counter of the billeting office. The renovated World War II building reminded me of Basic Combat Training from over ten years earlier at Fort McClellan, Alabama. I had enlisted to escape the confines and control of my first husband.

"Good afternoon," he said. "How can I help you?" He rearranged the paperwork and folders on his desk as if searching for something.

"I'm Sergeant First Class (SFC) Britt, the new NCOIC for the 10th Mountain Division Field Artillery Evaluation Team," I said.

"Ah, yes, SFC Britt…," he said, then turned a file toward me. "Please sign in here." He glanced at my registration. "Some colonel's been asking about your arrival," he said before assigning me quarters and handing me a map.

I approached the three-bedroom house and wondered if it had been a former officer's quarters from when Camp Edwards was in its heyday. I selected a bedroom, unpacked my bags, and checked out the rest of the building. The refrigerator was empty except for some sauce packets from a take-out restaurant. I found a laundry room located in the basement with some leftover detergent. As I came back upstairs, I heard a voice.

"Hello?" a man called through the open front door. "I'm Colonel Brown, who you'll be working for while you're here." He took a much-needed breath. "How are you?" He reached out a fleshy hand that held mine a little too long. *What had I gotten myself into?*

"I'm good. Thank you, Sir," I said as I recovered my hand.

He was slightly taller than my five-foot-five frame, overweight, balding, with a paunch. His smile seemed genuine. He wore a wedding band.

"Can we sit down and discuss the job?" He asked, not waiting for acknowledgment before marching to the dining room, where he sat down and opened the case.

I left the front door open because it made me feel more comfortable.

"You and I need to prepare the headquarters building for the evaluation teams' arrival in 30 days." He seemed rushed, as though it was happening tomorrow. I sat down as he pulled out various forms and documents to show me. And for the next two and a half hours, he droned on about everything we needed to do.

I stifled a yawn. It was getting late, the sun was setting, and after driving most of the day, I was beyond tired.

Just when I thought I couldn't keep my eyes open any longer, a woman moved into the quarters. She introduced herself as Captain Smith and told us she would be here for four weeks working on an assignment across the Post. I felt slightly more comfortable with someone else in that old house.

The Colonel stood, not to greet the Captain but to gather his things. "We can discuss this more tomorrow at the headquarters building," he said, pointing to a location on the map. "I'll see you there at 0800."

"Yes, Sir. Goodnight," I said, somewhat baffled. Had he decided to end our meeting because of my new housemate's arrival? Or had he just realized how late it had gotten?

"Goodnight," he said, and walked out the door.

Our new administrative headquarters was in an old office building with an enormous reception area that provided ample space for two clerks. The Colonel claimed the office next to the only bathroom.

I later learned that men generally ignored the sign on the door, attached with a string that read, "Men" on one side and "Women" on the other. Luckily, the latrine had enclosed stalls. As a result, I invariably found myself in the restroom with a man, which was generally a surprise to us both, but we just carried on.

I occupied a desk just outside the Colonel's office. Another desk was set up for my clerk, who was yet to be assigned, near the entrance to the building so that he/she could greet people as they arrived. We ordered, received, and set up all the office equipment and furniture necessary for the operation. The large room at the back of the building was designated for group meetings and as a classroom.

One evening, I hung out with some local civilian employees. We went to a Chinese Restaurant, and when I received my fortune cookie, it read, "You have to kiss a lot of frogs before you meet Prince Charming." I dismissed it with a laugh, but a small part of me was hopeful. I still believed in the possibility of true love.

As we waited for the first team to arrive, the Colonel and I would often go on long walks in the evenings for exercise, where we discussed everything from trivial topics to our marriages and relationships. We visited Boston one Saturday and had an enjoyable dinner together. We became friends of sorts.

During those first few weeks, he made it clear that he was interested in more than just a professional relationship, though I was not interested in more than friendship. He hadn't made any inappropriate advances toward me, but there were times when he seemed overly friendly and a little too earnest. Through it all, I tried to remain congenial and respectful. I wondered if he was just one of those soldiers who lived by the "What goes on TDY, stays on TDY" motto. I came to realize he was basically harmless.

About a week into our three-month tour, a clerk arrived. She was a small, slender, and somewhat nervous woman. When the Colonel commented on her work in a firm tone, she broke down and cried in front of him—in uniform. I was astounded and seriously embarrassed, knowing that some men judged all women based on the actions of a few. I dressed her down and advised that she never disgrace the uniform like that again. She was relieved of duty and replaced with a male corporal. This meant that I would be the only female in the office, as all the evaluators were field artillery—a specialty that was not open to women until 2015.

As the only woman, I encountered my share of attention. Most of it was harmless flirting, and after my recent breakup, the friendly banter soothed my broken heart just a little. Although I'd been in situations with men who crossed the line to vulgar, like most military women, I laughed it off. What choice did we have? Make a big deal about it, then be ostracized for the rest of the tour? "Sexual harassment" was not even acknowledged back then, and policies did not exist.

When the first team arrived, the Colonel and I were set up and ready for action like a well-oiled machine. We guided the first rotation of evaluators through the process and activities progressed without a hitch.

"One life is all we have and we live it as we believe in living it.
But to sacrifice what you are and to live without belief,
that is a fate more terrible than dying."
—Joan of Arc

## Chapter 15

# The Meeting

When the second rotation was in route, the civilian billeting officer called and said, "This has never happened before, but we have no accommodations on post for your team of evaluators. You'll have to contract rooms in a local motel."

I received authorization to book motel rooms before their arrival and changed the announcement board to reflect the names of the incoming team of evaluators.

The second team arrived generally as a group. "I have bad news and good news," I said. They looked skeptical. "There's no room at the inn, so you'll be in a motel in Falmouth for the duration of your TDY." A cheer sounded. I gave them their reservations, and they dispersed.

The team leader, a Major, came in separately from the others. "Hello, Sir, welcome," I said when he entered the office. "No rooms are available on post, so you'll be staying at the Falmouth Holiday Inn." I handed him the registration information.

"I'm Ed, by the way." He offered an electric smile that could dazzle even the most hardened heart and extended his hand in a succinct, professional manner. His attention to detail was evident in everything from his appropriately short blonde hair to his sparkling blue eyes. He stood out— not just because of his crisp uniform and gleaming boots, but because of how he carried himself, a blend of authority and approachability.

I grinned back.

The Colonel came out of his office, introduced himself, and extended his hand. "Hello, Major. I'm Colonel Brown. "How was your drive down here?"

"Hello, Sir," he said. "It was uneventful."

"Welcome. Let us know if you need anything."

"Alright, Sir. I will." They shook hands, and the Colonel went back to his office.

The Major sat in the chair next to my desk as I walked to the copier. "The last team told me to check you out," he said.

I stopped mid-step, turned, and said, "Oh, really? What did they say?"

"Just that you were efficient," he said.

"How do you pronounce your last name?" I asked, "Is the 'e' silent?"

"Yes," he said, "My mother used to say it rhymes with hell." He laughed.

I noticed his name was misspelled on the board, so I corrected it.

"What do you do around here for fun?" he asked.

"The Officer's Club is hosting a lobster dinner tonight," I offered.

"That sounds great."

"So, you'll go then?" I asked.

"Of course, "he said. "Wouldn't miss it. I'm going to check into the motel and change clothes. "I'll see you tonight?"

"Yes, absolutely," I said.

After he left, I went to post an announcement on the bulletin board. The Colonel exited his office and said, "Don't forget about the lobster dinner tonight." He leaned in closer to me and whispered, "Don't invite that Major."

I was happy to report, "Oh, I already did." He grumbled a little but didn't say anything more.

At dinner, something magical happened. As Ed regaled us with stories about growing up on his father's Florida orange grove and jokes about a fictional "Roadkill Restaurant," I found myself laughing uncontrollably. One by one, our dinner companions excused themselves—first Captain Smith's husband, who was visiting, then the captain herself, and finally the Colonel. He tried to talk to me, but I was so into Ed he finally scowled and said, "Well, I'll see you later." But Ed and I remained, lost in conversation that flowed as naturally as if we'd known each other for years. What started as shared laughter evolved into something much deeper. We discovered parallel lives—both Army veterans, survivors of failed marriages, both seeking something genuine.

After dinner, we moved from the dining room to the adjacent lounge. We gravitated toward each other, caught in a magnetic pull that felt both intoxicating and dangerous. Ed spoke of his military experiences, sharing tales of deployments that had tested his resolve and his faith, as well as moments of vulnerability that revealed the human beneath the uniform. He explained that he was an unwavering Roman Catholic.

As we continued to talk, I felt something shift within me—a blossoming realization that perhaps this connection was more than just a fleeting moment. There was an ease to our conversation, a rhythm that felt natural. Each lingering glance drew me deeper into the warmth of his presence.

When he reached across the table to brush his fingers against mine, the simple touch sent a jolt of electricity through me. I looked down at our hands, a delicate connection that felt both stimulating and terrifying. I felt vulnerable yet thrilled, as if I were teetering on the edge of something beautiful.

"Do you believe in fate?" he asked, his voice low and serious, pulling me back into the moment.

"I don't know," I admitted, my heart pounding at the thought he might be experiencing these same feelings. "But I think sometimes God has a way of bringing people together when they least expect it."

He smiled a slow, genuine smile that lit up his entire face. "I think you might be right." "You know, I wasn't supposed to be on the evaluation team this year. My commander said he'd find someone else to go. He did, but my replacement broke his leg last week. So here I am."

I couldn't help but think of my fortune cookie and wondered if this could be real. I didn't want to make the same mistake of rushing into anything, which had led to the instability and unfulfillment of the last four years.

At that moment, surrounded by the warmth of the lounge's fireplace and the possibilities that lay ahead, I felt a spark of hope igniting within me. This was just the beginning, and for the first time in a long while, I was eager to see where it might lead.

"I wasn't going to come here either," I said. "I asked my personnel office if there were any tours available. They told me Nova Scotia or Camp Edwards. Neither really interested me, so I said I would call back. The third time, after about six weeks, I called again and learned there was no change. When I asked where Camp Edwards was, the Sergeant said, 'Cape Cod.' That didn't sound too bad, so I said I'd take it."

"So, it really is fate that brought us together then," he said. We smiled at each other our eyes filled with longing.

"Two months ago, I was at the Warrant Officer Academy, but my duffel bag didn't arrive with me. After two days, with no bags in sight, I knew I was too far behind the training curve, so I requested to leave."

"I'm sorry that didn't work out for you. You would make an excellent Warrant Officer, but if you'd stayed, maybe we wouldn't have met," he said.

We left the club together, and in the parking lot, under the stars, his kiss ignited a fire I thought had long since burned out. Our connection transcended the physical; it was spiritual, emotional, and intellectual-a perfect storm of compatibility that left me breathless. Only one night, and I was already into this guy. I was afraid, based on my past experiences, that good things never lasted. I felt it had to slow down a bit, but it didn't. We were together that night and as much as possible through the end of his rotation at Camp Edwards.

The next morning, we went to a cafe on post for breakfast. We sat across from each other, the clinking of cups and the low murmur of conversations forming a cozy backdrop. I watched him as he took a sip of his coffee, his lips curling slightly around the rim of the mug, and I felt a flutter in my chest, a giddy mix of anticipation and nervousness.

"You know," he said, setting the cup down with a gentle thud, "I used to think coffee was just a caffeine fix. But now, it feels like a ritual. Like sharing a moment." His eyes sparkled with sincerity, and I found myself leaning closer, drawn by the warmth of his words.

I smiled, tucking a stray hair behind my ear, feeling the weight of his gaze. "I used to drink it just to stay awake," I confessed, my voice barely above a whisper. "But now… I think I'm starting to appreciate the little things."

He nodded, his expression encouraging, and the corners of his mouth tilted up in a way that made my heart race. "It's funny how the simplest things can change," he replied, tracing his finger along the rim of his mug. "Like how a cup of coffee can turn into a beautiful moment with someone you've just met."

I could feel the air around us crackling with an unspoken connection, something dramatic and real. The way he spoke, with a softness that made me feel safe, sent shivers down my spine. He leaned back in his chair, his presence both calming and exhilarating, and I couldn't help but notice the way the light danced in his hair and the way his laughter filled the spaces between us.

"If you could be anyone else in the world, who would you want to be, and why?" he asked his eyes sparkling with curiosity.

I hesitated, the weight of my past swirling around in my mind, but something about his gaze urged me to share. "I would be you." I paused. "Because you seem to really have your life together and you know where you are going."

He leaned forward, his elbows resting on the table, completely engrossed. "You're joking, right?"

I paused, searching for the right words. "No, I'm being totally honest. You seem happy and satisfied with your life and know how to get where you want to go." I caught his eye, and the intensity of our connection sent a thrill through me.

"Maybe we should consider going there together," he suggested, a playful smile dancing on his lips. My heart skipped at the thought, and a flutter of excitement filled the space between us.

"Maybe we should," I replied, the words spilling out before I could think twice.

There was a rhythm to our friendship, an unspoken understanding that transcended rank. Whenever we were outside, in uniform, I saluted him, but he just folded into laughter and never returned it. I was happy he was not in my chain of command, so concerns about fraternization were limited. Each moment crackled with unacknowledged tension, a shared secret that both thrilled and terrified me.

As I gazed into his eyes, I wondered if he felt it, too. The world outside was fraught with challenges, deployments looming, responsibilities heavy—but in our stolen moments, we crafted a sanctuary. I was drawn to his strength, yet it was his vulnerability that truly captivated me. He was not just an Army Major; he was a man navigating the same uncertainties I faced, and in that journey, we began to forge something profoundly inexplicable.

Over the following weeks, we spent our free time exploring Cape Cod towns, singing songs from decades past, and going for dinner and drinks. At one lounge, we both ordered mixed drinks. The waiter said, "Oh, alright. I'll have to card you." Ed and I looked at each other and we burst into laughter. We were still laughing when the waiter returned with our drinks. At Woods Hole, we sat in an elegant restaurant on the water, so lost in each other's eyes that I can't remember if we ate anything.

Our relationship deepened during our weekends together. We were so comfortable around each other, and building a repertoire of shared experiences was pure joy. The first Friday after Ed left Camp Edwards, he flew back down. We saw the movie *Ghost*, whose intensely romantic theme song, "Unchained Melody," became our song. We also went to Boston for a Roger Whittaker concert, whom we both love.

"Let's meet halfway between your duty station and mine next weekend," I suggested.

"Sounds like a winner," he agreed. When we were at dinner, we talked about everything. Suddenly, he said, "I want you to call me George, my middle name, reserved only for those closest to me."

"Okay…George," I said, trying it out. "I want to learn more about Catholicism," I said, knowing how important his faith was to him. I had been raised Lutheran, but I drifted away from the church after they changed their Sunday service format in search of something more like what I remembered from my childhood. We visited a religious bookstore and stocked up on reading material for both of us.

When we attended Mass that weekend, as incense wafted over the sanctuary and lyrical Latin verses filled my ears, I was surprised to discover that the Catholic service was what I'd been longing for. As I sat in the pew, I envisioned myself walking down the aisle in a white wedding dress—though I kept it to myself.

The Friday before my tour at Camp Edwards came to an end, fate intervened. I received a call from the Tennessee State Personnel Office.

"Your name has come up on the register for employment as a Parole Officer," a man with an authoritative voice said. "You need to report on Monday."

"I'm currently on active military duty, which ends in three days," I said. "I can be there next Monday."

His response was rather shocking. "Either you show up in Tennessee on Monday, or you're off the employment register." This meant no opportunities for any other position. I hung up the phone, frustrated by the injustice of it all. It reminded me of the Tennessee "good ole' boy network," like when I had applied for a management position and was told I would have to be hired on as a secretary before consideration for leadership, despite having a college degree. Yet there was nothing I could do. The Uniformed Services Employment and Reemployment Act, which might have protected me, wasn't enacted until a few years later.

During one of our weekend rendezvous in Upstate New York, Ed and I were in the coffee shop on post. After researching the want ads in the local newspaper, I said, "Oh, look, I could qualify for these three positions."

Ed looked surprised and hesitantly asked, "Are you considering moving here?"

"Well, the thought crossed my mind," I said. "In Tennessee, I'm not only homeless, but I also have no job prospects."

"Really?" He was incredulous. "That would be wonderful," he said. "I can help you move."

Faced with the choice between trying to end my tour early to take a job as a Tennessee Parole Officer or following my heart to Upstate New York, I chose love. Ed helped me move to a cute apartment near a mall, and I found work directing a teen runaway program while pursuing my first master's degree in psychology.

Ed's Christmas Day proposal later that year led to an April 1991 wedding, followed by a formal ceremony in Florida, where my vision came true—and I walked down the aisle in a lovely white wedding gown.

My natural optimism and the bit of romantic hope I still carried had been sparked by that silly fortune cookie, which turned out to be right. George used the word "fate" on that first night together; I'm reminded of the quote, "Fortune favors the bold." With all of my past mistakes and pattern of self-neglect, my story does have its bold moments. I had come a long way from the words "Don't come back." I left anyway. I learned the importance of getting to know the right person by building trust, compatibility, and emotional connection. I finally learned to honor myself, and that's when fate smiled on that handsome major and me.

# Epilogue

You may be wondering if there is a "post" complex post-traumatic stress disorder—a day when you arrive on the other side of the mountain that you've been climbing to get yourself far away from the "bottom" where your experiences turned into gaping wounds that have been anything but easy to heal. While the clean air on this side of the mountain is refreshing and all the wildflowers seem more vibrant, the past is still a part of me, as is yours a part of who you are. It's up to you whether you will use it or let it use you. I have, thank goodness, found ways to use it to bring positivity, healing, and hope to myself and many people, including you and other dear readers of this book. For me, this side of C-PTSD is beautiful. It took a lot of willingness to face the truth, courage to make profound changes, a decision to lean on faith in God, and a new heart open to a completely new kind of love.

Ed and I married in April of 1991. I completed my Master's Degree in Human Services (Counseling) in 1992, then earned a Master's Degree in Clinical Psychology, and a doctorate in Clinical Psychology from Argosy University in Honolulu in 2001. I completed my internship at American Lake Veterans Administration Hospital, Tacoma, Washington. Then I began working as a Forensic Psychologist for an all-male population of "Not Guilty by Reason of Insanity" (NGRI) in Tacoma. I retired in 2008. Ed and I both love the unique landscapes and mild winters of the Sonoran Desert in Arizona, where we live with "J.P.," our Goldendoodle.

My life after my two divorces has not been all peaches and cream by any stretch of the imagination. I've had periods of feeling abandoned, which my husband has dealt with head-on by patiently talking over the issue with me and showing understanding. I am still hypervigilant and experience exaggerated reactions to being surprised. Sometimes my anger rises up from an old place and bursts on the scene uninvited. One time, I kicked a box so hard it flew through two rooms in my home, just because of my frustration when I couldn't easily open it. Another time, I swiped a medicine chest full of medications onto the floor with a violent swing of my arm. My husband quietly and calmly cleaned up the mess I had made.

When I was married to both my first and second husbands, I was mentally "packing to leave" all of the time. When we were driving around, I'd see For Rent signs and would think, *Oh, I could leave him and live there.* I always told myself, *He doesn't love me… I'm unlovable.* I still take medications for depression, anxiety, and insomnia, all of which help my moods to stay on an even keel. There are days when I feel really down and think I'm no good to anyone. Those times are now fewer and further between. Mostly, I get to breathe fresh air, clean and free of past traumas.

I tend to be an introvert and don't go out among people very often because it makes me nervous. I do enjoy some communities very much—I'm a member of a local veteran's group and a local women veteran's organization. I feel so strongly about my mission to help women, especially those with C-PTSD, that I am seeking speaking opportunities where I can make a difference for the right audience. I also enjoy being a guest on podcasts that are topical to recovery, psychology, PTSD, and women's empowerment.

I support the Tunnels to Towers Foundation and two Catholic churches. I also support the National Center for PTSD, the C-PTSD Foundation, RAINN (Rape, Abuse, and Incest National Network), Take Back the Night (TBTN), and the American Society for the Positive Care of Children (ASPCC).

So, the bottom line is that you always live with the symptoms of Complex PTSD. And, you have a choice about your daily focus—the present is where your happiness is accessible, not the past. You and your mate just need to continuously work on leaving the past in the past, and deal with triggering situations as they arise. Addressing concerns openly is very beneficial because communication is key to getting through them gracefully.

As we celebrated our thirty-fourth anniversary in 2025, I realized that true love isn't just about finding someone who makes you laugh or shares your interests. It's about discovering someone who intuitively understands your thoughts before they are spoken, respects and embraces your strengths and vulnerabilities, and shares your vision of the future.

# Appendix A

# Causes, Symptoms, and Statistics

### Adverse Childhood Experience (ACE)

(The ACES Quiz was developed by the CDC and Kaiser Permanente. The quiz is copyright-free.)

About sixty-four percent of adults reported at least one Adverse Child Experience (ACE), which can include exposure to violence, abuse, or neglect; a death by suicide in the family; substance use or dependence in the family; mental health disorders in the family; having a family member incarcerated; chronic poverty or neglect; housing instability; or growing up in a crime-heavy environment. One in six reported experiencing four or more ACEs.

Post-Traumatic Stress Disorder (PTSD) is a psychiatric disorder that can develop after a person experiences a traumatic event. Complex or C-PTSD can result if a person experiences prolonged or repeated trauma over months or years, like childhood sexual abuse.

Childhood sexual abuse is a serious health problem and an Adverse Childhood Experience (ACE). It can have a long-term impact on health, opportunity, and well-being. At least one in four girls and one in twenty boys in the United States experience child sexual abuse.

About ninety percent of child sexual abuse is perpetrated by someone known and trusted by the child or child's family members. Experiencing child sexual abuse can affect how a person thinks, acts, and feels over a lifetime. This can result in short- and long-term physical, mental, and behavioral health consequences, such as physical health issues, sexually transmitted infections (STIs), physical injuries, and chronic conditions later in life including heart disease, obesity, and cancer. Even decades after the abuse, people may experience depression, PTSD, and behavioral consequences of risky behaviors. Examples of those are: substance use/misuse, including alcohol and opioids, promiscuity leading to STIs or unwanted pregnancy, hanging around unsafe or abusive people, or turning to suicide or suicide attempts.

Experiencing child sexual abuse can also increase a person's risk for future victimization. As reported in RAINN (Rape, Abuse & Incest National Network), women who experienced child sexual abuse are at a two to thirteen times increased risk for experiencing sexual violence in adulthood. And, people who experienced child sexual abuse are at twice the risk of experiencing non-sexual intimate partner violence.

## Diagnosing C-PTSD

Complex PTSD does not appear in the Diagnostic & Statistical Manual of Mental Disorders, 5th Edition (DSM-V) by the American Psychiatric Association, but does appear in the World Health Organization (WHO) as a distinct diagnosis in its Classification of Diseases (ICD-11)

Many clinicians recognize C-PTSD as a separate condition because the traditional PTSD diagnosis does not fully capture the unique symptoms of individuals who have experienced prolonged, repeated trauma.

## Some Causal Effects of Depression

Emotional Eating: Children who have experienced sexual abuse may develop maladaptive coping strategies, including emotional eating. Food can serve as a source of comfort or distraction from trauma memories or fears, leading to weight gain and even more shame. This is something I personally experienced. I used food to self-soothe and cope with anxiety, depression, and feelings of worthlessness, and my overeating became a habit I had no control over. Three different times in my life I turned to food for "help" and each time gained over 100 pounds.

Survivors of sexual abuse may struggle with body image and self-esteem, which could manifest in unhealthy eating habits. Some might engage in extreme dieting, which was what I did in 1989, and became anorexic for about two years.

Childhood trauma can cause dysregulation of the hypothalamic-pituitary-adrenal (HPA) axis, affecting stress hormones like cortisol. Elevated cortisol levels are associated with increased appetite and fat storage, particularly in the abdominal area. A chronic state of stress and trauma may influence metabolic processes, potentially leading to weight gain or difficulties in maintaining a healthy weight.

Survivors of childhood sexual abuse may feel isolated or stigmatized, which can lead to social withdrawal. Reduced physical activity due to isolation can contribute to weight gain. The environment in which a child grows up after experiencing abuse can play a role. A nice, normal family develops coping mechanisms, too. For example, if a family turns to unhealthy eating as a way to deal with stress or anxiety, this can be detrimental to a child's relationship with food. Of course, other forms of addiction (i.e., anything that serves as an escape from reality) in the household can impact a child, including alcohol, drugs, pornography, shopping/overspending, gambling, and so forth.

The ramifications of childhood sexual abuse often extend into adulthood, influencing eating behaviors, body image, weight, sexuality, substance abuse, and physical ailments later in life. The relationship between childhood sexual abuse and weight gain is multifaceted, involving emotional, psychological, physiological, and social dimensions. It is important for survivors to have access to appropriate psychological support and nutritional guidance to address these complex issues in a healthy manner.

**Effects on Brain Development**

Childhood sexual abuse can have profound and lasting effects on brain development, leading to a range of psychological, emotional, and cognitive challenges. Research indicates that such traumatic experiences can disrupt normal brain development in several ways.

Chronic exposure to trauma activates the body's stress response system, particularly involving the hypothalamic-pituitary-adrenal (HPA) axis. This can lead to an overproduction of stress hormones, such as cortisol, which, when persistently elevated, may damage brain structures integral to emotional regulation and memory, including the hippocampus and prefrontal cortex.

During childhood, the brain is particularly plastic, meaning it develops in response to environmental stimuli. Traumatic experiences can alter neural pathways and brain structure, potentially leading to maladaptive coping mechanisms, increased anxiety, depression, and difficulty in forming healthy relationships later in life.

Trauma can disrupt brain regions involved in emotional regulation, such as the amygdala. This may lead to heightened fear responses, challenges in emotional expression, and difficulties maintaining stable relationships.

Childhood trauma has been associated with impairments in attention, memory, and executive functioning. Children may struggle with concentration, decision-making, and impulse control due to disruptions in their neural circuitry.

Long-term effects of childhood sexual abuse can manifest as various mental health disorders, including post-traumatic stress disorder (PTSD), anxiety, depression, and personality disorders. These conditions can stem from alterations in brain regions responsible for regulating mood, cognition, and behavior.

Understanding the impact of childhood sexual abuse on brain development underscores the importance of trauma-informed care. Therapeutic approaches should aim to address not only the emotional and psychological needs of survivors but also the neurobiological effects of their trauma. Interventions that incorporate mindfulness, cognitive-behavioral therapy (CBT), and somatic experiencing can be beneficial in promoting healing and resilience.

Overall, addressing the complex relationship between childhood sexual abuse and brain development is crucial for supporting survivors in their recovery journey and promoting healthier outcomes in adulthood.

**Symptoms of Complex PTSD May Include:**

- Difficulty controlling emotions
- Feeling very angry or distrustful towards the world
- Constant feelings of emptiness or hopelessness
- Feeling as if you are permanently damaged or worthless
- Feeling as if you are completely different from other people
- Feeling like nobody can understand what happened to you
- Avoiding people and places

- Often experiencing dissociative symptoms such as depersonalization or derealization
- Regular suicidal feelings
- Flashbacks
- Hypervigilance
- Lapses in memory
- Self-harm or cutting
- Distorted sense of self
- Autoimmune ailments
- Risky sexual behavior
- Headaches or migraines
- Unable to regulate emotions
- Stomach and gastrointestinal issues
- Nightmares and sleep disturbance
- Poor interpersonal relationships
- Character flaws such as chronic lying
- Drug and alcohol abuse
- Self-blame or low self-esteem
- Mental and physical health issues
- Self-destructive behaviors
- Lack of feeling
- Poor concentration
- Hopelessness
- Apathy
- Mistrust
- Dissociation

## What Causes Complex PTSD?

- Childhood abuse, neglect, or abandonment

- Ongoing domestic violence or abuse
- Repeatedly witnessing violence and abuse
- Being forced or manipulated into prostitution
- Torture, kidnapping, or slavery
- Being a prisoner of war

**You Are More Likely to Develop Complex PTSD if:**

- You experienced trauma at an early age
- The trauma lasted for a long time
- Escape or rescue was unlikely or impossible
- You have experienced multiple traumas
- You were harmed by someone close to you
- You told no one what was happening, or your telling fell on deaf ears

**Blind Spots**

"Blind spots" refers to a psychological defense mechanism in which the traumatized individual is unable or unwilling to see and process the full impact of the harm they experienced. It is an unconscious coping strategy that helps the mind avoid overwhelming anxiety or pain, but it can impede healing and personal growth.

**Dissociation**

Dissociation, or not recognizing what was going on right in front of me, is a psychological phenomenon where an individual experiences a disconnection between thoughts, identity, consciousness, memory, and perception. It can manifest in various ways, including:

- Emotional numbness: Difficulty recognizing or responding to feelings, leading to a sense of emotional blunting or a lack of emotional reactivity.
- Depersonalization: Feeling detached from one's own body, thoughts, or feelings, as if observing them from outside or as if they are not truly their own.

- Derealization: Experiencing the external world as unreal, distorted, foggy, or dreamlike.

- Memory difficulties: Problems recalling specific events, personal information, or even stretches of time.

- Overthinking: Getting caught in loops of negative thoughts about the past or worries about the future, leading to difficulty focusing on the present moment.

- Self-image concerns: Excessive worry about how one is perceived by others, or struggling with feelings of inadequacy or "imposter syndrome."

Dissociation and emotional numbness can be a way the mind deals with overwhelming stress or trauma, especially those experienced during childhood.

If these feelings are persistent, severe, or interfere with daily life, it's crucial to seek professional support from a doctor or mental health professional to explore potential underlying causes and develop appropriate coping strategies or treatment plans.

Untreated dissociation and emotional numbness can lead to difficulties in relationships, work, and other areas of life, and may increase the risk of other mental health issues or unhealthy coping behaviors. In essence, living "in one's head" in a dissociative state can be a challenging experience marked by a sense of unreality, emotional detachment, and difficulty engaging with the present moment.

*Derealization* (the sense of unreality or detachment from the external world, where surroundings may seem dreamlike or distorted) describes my lack of ability to recognize when my sister was being molested at night in our bedroom. Three feet away. With my eyes and ears open.

My brain wouldn't let it register. My mind still won't let me remember anything about it.

## Love Bombing

"Love bombing" is a manipulation tactic often employed in the early phase of a romantic relationship, where one individual showers another with excessive affection, attention, and praise. It's like providing an all-you-can-eat buffet to someone who is hungry (or starving) for something to meet an unfulfilled emotional need. This over-generous behavior is designed to gain control over the other person, creating an intense emotional bond.

Key characteristics of love bombing include excessive praise and attention. The love bomber expresses overwhelming admiration, compliments, and affection, often making grand gestures that seem sincere but may be superficial. The love bomber is intent on "sweeping you off your feet" and pushes for fast emotional closeness. Much too soon, they profess their "love."

Once a bond is established, the love bomber may attempt to isolate the recipient from friends, family, and support systems to increase dependency on them. Initial affection may be followed by withdrawal or coldness, creating a cycle of highs and lows. This inconsistency can leave the recipient feeling confused and desperate to regain the intimacy they once shared. Except that it's not real intimacy. Love bombing is, in part, a process of making a person dependent on the euphoric dopamine and endorphin boost they experience when it's being done.

As a matter of manipulation, the love bomber may use guilt, flattery, or intimidation to maintain control. They often frame their affection in a way that makes the recipient feel responsible for the love bomber's happiness. Unrealistic expectations are used as pressure to gain higher and higher levels of compliance, affection, and attention. Some potential consequences include emotional dependency: The excessive affection and dopamine hits can create a strong emotional and physical attachment, making it difficult for the recipient to leave the relationship despite toxicity or danger.

The manipulation may lead to feelings of inadequacy if the recipient feels they can't meet the love bomber's unrealistic demands. The emotional rollercoaster of psychological stress contributes to anxiety, depression, and feelings of confusion, as the recipient struggles to understand the relationship dynamics.

Recognizing the game and protecting your personal boundaries in a love bombing situation involves several strategies to maintain emotional safety and well-being.

- Notice the Signs: Awareness is key. Love bombers often overwhelm you with affection and may pressure you into a rapid relationship progression. Recognizing these behaviors early can help you take a step back.

- Define Your Boundaries: Clearly articulate your boundaries regarding time, emotional availability, and physical intimacy. Know what you are comfortable with and what makes you feel rushed or pressured. A person who is smitten and overly attentive may be innocent of manipulative love-bombing; a good way to tell if that's not their control game is if they respect your boundaries once you make them very clear.

- Communicate Openly: Don't hesitate to express your feelings and concerns. Let your partner know if their affection feels overwhelming or if you need space. Healthy relationships thrive on open dialogue and respecting one another's feelings.

- Slow Down: If you feel rushed, intentionally slow down the pace of the relationship. Spending less time together allows you to evaluate the dynamics and assess your feelings without pressure.

- Seek Support from Friends and Family: Share your experiences with trusted friends or family members. They can provide perspective and support, helping you stay grounded and confident in your choices. You may be in the throes of a "love addiction" and should not expect yourself to handle everything all alone.

- Trust Your Instincts: Pay attention to your gut feelings. If something feels off, take a moment to reflect on your emotions. Trusting your instincts can help you identify actions that violate your boundaries. Practice Self-Care: Engage in activities that promote your well-being and self-esteem. Spending time alone or focusing on personal interests reinforces your sense of identity and your ability to maintain boundaries.

- Educate Yourself: Understanding the psychology behind love bombing can empower you. Familiarize yourself with manipulation tactics, "love" addiction, and emotional abuse to recognize and respond effectively.

- Set Consequences: If your boundaries are repeatedly disrespected, you must establish consequences. Whatever you keep putting up with will never change. Take a break from the relationship to reevaluate its dynamics.

- Seek Professional Help: If you find yourself feeling overwhelmed, consider seeking the guidance of a therapist or counselor. They can provide strategies to reinforce your boundaries and cope with emotional manipulation.

By implementing these strategies, you can protect your personal boundaries and foster healthier relationships that prioritize mutual respect and emotional safety.

# Appendix B

# Studies and More Information

### Rape, Abuse, & Incest National Network (RAINN) Statistics

Ninety-four percent of women who are raped experience symptoms of PTSD during the two weeks following the rape. (D.S. Riggs, T. Murdock, W. Walsh, A prospective examination of post-traumatic stress disorder in rape victims. Journal of Traumatic Stress 355-475 (1992).

Thirty percent of women report symptoms of PTSD nine months after a rape. (J. R. T. Davidson & E. B. Foa (Eds.) Post-Traumatic Stress Disorder: DSM-IV and Beyond. American Psychiatric Press: Washington, DC (pp. 23-36).

Following sexual assault, survivors are more likely to abuse drugs: 3.4 times more likely to use marijuana; 6 times more likely to use cocaine; 10 times more likely to use other major drugs. DG Kilpatrick, CN Edmunds, AK Seymour, Rape in America: A Report to the Nation. Arlington, VA: National Center and Medical University of South Carolina (1992).

Approximately seventy percent of rape or sexual assault victims experience moderate to severe distress, a larger percentage for any other violent crime. (Department of Justice, Office of Justice Programs, Bureau of Justice Statistics, Socio-emotional Impact of Violent Crime (2014).

Eighty-four percent of victims experience moderate to severe distress when victimized by an intimate partner. (Justice, Office of Justice Programs, Bureau of Justice Statistics, Socio-emotional Impact of Violent Crime (2014).

Seventy-nine percent of survivors experience moderate to severe distress when victimized by a family member, close friend, or acquaintance. (Department of Justice, Office of Justice Programs, Bureau of Justice Statistics, Socio-emotional Impact of Violent Crime (2014).

Sixty-seven percent of survivors experience moderate to severe distress when victimized by a stranger. (Department of Justice, Office of Justice Programs, Bureau of Justice Statistics, Socio-emotional Impact of Violent Crime (2014).

Thirty-seven percent of survivors experience problems with family members and friends, including getting into arguments more frequently than before, not being able to trust their loved ones, or not feeling as close to them as before the crime. (Department of Justice, Office of Justice Programs, Bureau of Justice Statistics, Socio-emotional Impact of Violent Crime (2014).

Thirty-eight percent of survivors of sexual violence experience school or work problems, which can include significant problems with a boss, coworker, or peer. (Department of Justice, Office of Justice Programs, Bureau of Justice Statistics, Socio-emotional Impact of Violent Crimes (2014).

Between 2009-2013, Child Protective Services substantiated or found strong evidence that 63,000 children a year were sexually abused. (Department of Health and Human Services, Administration for Children and Families, Administration of Children, Youth and Families, Children's Bureau, Child Maltreatment Survey, 2012 (2013).

Every 74 seconds someone in the US is sexually assaulted. Every nine minutes that someone is a child. (Department of Justice, Office of Justice Programs, Bureau of Justice Statistics, National Crime Victimization Survey, 2019-2022).

An estimated 423,020 people aged 12+ experience sexual violence each year. (Department of Justice, Office of Justice Programs, Bureau of Justice Statistics, Sex Offenses and Offenders, 1997)

Ninety-three percent of victims under 18 know their abuser. Of sexual abuse cases reported to law enforcement, ninety-three percent of juvenile victims knew the perpetrator; fifty-nine percent were acquaintances; thirty-four percent were family members, and only seven percent were strangers to the victim. (Department of Justice, Office of Justice Programs, Bureau of Justice Statistics, Sexual Assault of Young Children as Reported to Law Enforcement, 2000).

Sixty percent of rapes are committed by someone known to the victim. Thirty-one percent are committed by strangers; Nearly twenty-nine percent are committed by well-known or casual acquaintances; over twenty-one percent are committed by intimate partners; thirteen percent are committed by other relatives; almost four percent are committed by an unknown number of perpetrators; over two percent are committed by someone with an unknown relationship to the victim. (Department of Justice, Office of Justice Programs, Bureau of Justice Statistics, National Crime Victimization Survey, 2010-2016 (2017). Criminal Victimization, 2023).

Sixty-nine percent of sexual assault victims are between the ages of 12-34. Fifteen percent of victims are ages 12-17; fifty-four percent are 18-34. (Department of Justice, Office of Justice Programs, Bureau of Justice Statistics, Sex Offenses and Offenders (1997).

Eighty-two percent of all juvenile sexual assault victims are female. Ninety percent of adult rape victims are female. (Department of Justice, Office of Justice Programs, Bureau of Justice Statistics, Sexual Assault of Young Children as Reported to Law Enforcement (2000).

**Facts and Statistics (RAINN)**

+ Child abuse is of epidemic proportions

+ Child sexual abuse is preventable

+ Adults are responsible for ensuring that children have safe, stable, nurturing relationships and environments.

+ Childhood sexual abuse can have a long-term impact on health, opportunity, and well-being.

+ At least one in four girls and one in 20 boys in the United States experience child sexual abuse.

+ About ninety percent of child sexual abuse is perpetrated by someone known and trusted by the child or child's family members.

+ Experiencing child sexual abuse can affect how a person thinks, acts, and feels over a lifetime.

+ This can result in short- and long-term physical, mental, and behavioral health consequences as well as relationship difficulties throughout the lifespan.

+ People who experienced child sexual abuse are at twice the risk of experiencing non-sexual intimate partner violence.

+ Resources for child sexual abuse have mostly focused on treatment for victims and criminal justice-oriented approaches for people who commit child sexual abuse. These efforts are important after child sexual abuse has occurred. However, little investment has been made in preventing childhood sexual abuse.

+ Until recently, there have been few effective evidence-based strategies available to proactively protect children from child sexual abuse.

+ More resources are needed to develop, evaluate, disseminate, and implement evidence-based child sexual abuse primary prevention strategies.

+ These strategies can help ensure that all children have safe, stable, nurturing relationships and environments.

+ What the CDC is doing: CDC surveillance systems, violence prevention initiatives, and efforts to support partners in the field have increased our understanding of child sexual abuse. However, there are still critical gaps.

+ Additional efforts in child sexual abuse prevention are needed to:

Improve surveillance systems and data collection for monitoring child sexual abuse.

Increase our understanding of risk and protective factors for child sexual abuse perpetration and victimization.

Strengthen existing and develop new evidence-based policies, programs, and practices for the primary prevention of child sexual abuse through rigorous evaluation research.

Increase dissemination and implementation of evidence-based strategies for child sexual abuse prevention.

+ The CDC has developed Prevention Resources for Action, formerly known as "technical packages," to help states and communities utilize the best available evidence to prevent various types of violence.

+ Since 2020, the CDC has funded nine research cooperative agreements focused on the primary prevention of child sexual abuse. These research studies include both policy and program evaluations at the community, state, and national levels. These studies support the vision of a violence-free society in which all people and communities are safe, healthy, and free of childhood sexual abuse.

## Domestic Violence

Domestic violence is a significant social issue, and statistics reveal alarming patterns regarding its prevalence, demographic factors, and impacts. Here are some key statistics regarding domestic violence:

**Prevalence:** According to the World Health Organization (WHO), approximately 1 in 3 women globally have experienced physical or sexual violence by an intimate partner or sexual violence by a non-partner at some point in their lives.

**Men as Victims**: While women are disproportionately affected, men can also be victims of domestic violence. The National Coalition Against Domestic Violence (NCADV) states that about 1 in 4 men have experienced some form of physical violence by an intimate partner.

**Impact on Children**: Children exposed to domestic violence are at higher risk of experiencing emotional and behavioral problems. The U.S. Department of Justice reports that children witness about fifty percent of domestic violence incidents.

**Lethality**: Domestic violence can escalate to lethal outcomes. The National Domestic Violence Hotline (https://www.thehotline.org) indicates that about seventy-six percent of intimate partner homicides involve a gun.

**Accessibility:** A significant number of victims do not report the violence. The U.S. Bureau of Justice Statistics notes that less than twenty-five percent of domestic violence incidents are reported to the police.

**Economic Impact**: The economic cost of intimate partner violence is substantial. The Centers for Disease Control and Prevention (CDC) estimates that the cost, including medical services, mental health care, and lost productivity, exceeds $3 billion annually in the U.S. alone.

**Gender Disparities**: Women experience more severe forms of violence and are more likely to suffer injuries compared to men. Research shows that women are often at a higher risk of being killed by an intimate partner than men.

**Lifetime Experiences**: According to a National Intimate Partner and Sexual Violence Survey (NISVS), around thirty-six percent of women and twenty-nine percent of men have experienced some form of physical violence by an intimate partner during their lifetime.

**Substance Abuse Link**: There is a significant correlation between domestic violence and substance abuse. Studies indicate that alcohol and drug abuse can exacerbate the frequency and severity of domestic violence incidents.

**Impact of the Pandemic**: The COVID-19 pandemic has led to an increase in domestic violence incidents as lockdowns and restrictions left many victims trapped with their abusers. Reports of domestic violence calls increased significantly in several regions.

These statistics underline the critical need for awareness, resources, and support systems to combat domestic violence effectively and provide assistance to victims.

# GET HELP NOW

If you are experiencing intimate partner violence, including sexual assault or coercion, help is available by reaching out to one of these resources:

**The National Domestic Violence Hotline**: 1-800-799-SAFE (7233) or text START to 87788. (https://www.thehotline.org)

**The National Sexual Assault Hotline (RAINN):** 1-800-656-HOPE (4673) (https://rainn.org)

**Strong Hearts Native Helpline**: 1-844-7NATIVE (762-8483) (https://strongheartshelpline.org)

**Love is Respect**: Text "Lovels" to 22522 or call 1-866-331-9474 (https://loveisrespect.org)

**Victim Connect:** 1-855-4VICTIM (855-484-2846 (https://victimconnect.org)

**The Network/La Red**: 1-800-832-1901 (for LGBTQ+, kink, and polyamorous individuals) (https://tnlr.org)

# NARCISSISM AND MISOGYNY

Studies have consistently shown a significant correlation, suggesting that misogyny can be a component of narcissistic personality, although they are two distinct concepts. The link is especially associated with entitlement, a key factor in narcissism. The connection can be understood by examining how core narcissistic traits manifest in relationships with women.

Need for superiority and control – where they feel justified in pressuring or manipulating women into sexual intimacy and reacting with rage to rejection.

Response to female accomplishment – narcissistic men feel threatened by anything that challenges their own status, they may act with disdain to a partner's accomplishments. A misogynistic narcissistic man may feel deeply "emasculated" by a successful female partner as it disrupts his traditional belief in a submissive woman and threatens his own inflated ego.

Projected Unresolved Issues – some misogynistic behavior can stem from unresolved experiences with women in a narcissist's past, which he may then project on to all women.

Narcissistic men often exhibit a "Madonna-whore" complex, dividing women into either pure, nurturing figures or manipulative, promiscuous ones. This black and white thinking allows them to devalue women who don't conform to their prescribed roles.

# Resources

For individuals seeking help or more information about sexual violence and abuse:

**Take Back The Night (TBTN)** "Dear Katie" Survivor Support Podcast: 1-224-522-5998. Their global mission as a charitable foundation is to end all forms of violence, including sexual assault, sexual abuse, trafficking, stalking, gender harassment, and relationship violence, and to support survivors in their healing journey.

**American SPCC-The American Society for the Positive Care of Children** is a nonprofit organization focused on preventing child maltreatment by supporting parents and caregivers. (https://americanspcc.org)

**CPSD Foundation** is a 100 percent non-profit organization providing support to survivors of complex trauma. (https://cpsdfoundation.org)

**Dr. Marie Cosgrove - Resilience Strategist & Speaker**. (https://drcosgrove.com)

**Our Rescue (Child Trafficking: Education, Prevention, Rescue)** (https://ourrescue.org)

# Recommended Reading

The following books are highly recommended for additional information about dealing with trauma, including sexual violence and abuse:

*In An Unspoken Voice: How the Body Releases Trauma & Restores Goodness* by Peter A. Levine, PhD

*Complex PTSD: From Surviving to Thriving* by Pete Walker, MA, LMFT

*What Happened to You?* By Oprah Winfrey

*One Little Pill* by Deb Lawless Miller

*The Courage to Heal Workbook* by Laura Davis

*The Courage to Heal: A Guide for Women Survivors of Child Sexual Abuse* by Laura Davis and Ellen Bass

*The Sexual Healing Journey: A Guide for Survivors of Sexual Abuse*, 3rd Edition by Wendy Maltz, LCSW, DST

*The TAO of Trauma Healing: 12 Step Guide to Overcoming Anxiety and Depression* by Dr. Christy Walter

*You Are Not Your Trauma* by Caroline Beidler, MSW

# Acknowledgements

I'd like to thank Brooke Warner from She Writes Press, and instructor of "Write Your Memoir in Six Months," and Memoir Nation for her assistance and feedback in writing this book.

I'd like to acknowledge Stephanie Chandler, CEO of Nonfiction Author's Association, for the numerous courses she teaches with such eagerness, and for her enthusiastic support, as well as excelling at leading two sessions per month, which include Author Brainstorm Exchange and Group Roundtable Discussion.

A **GIANT** THANK YOU to Barbara Dee, my Editor and Publisher, for such a smooth and painless transition from rough copy to finalized publication, and all of the time and extensive work she did to get this book in print. Her team at Suncoast Digital Press is top-notch.

I commend my husband, Ed, for putting up with me writing at all hours of the night and day. And for his wisdom and heartfelt encouragement, strength, and support throughout the entire process.

# About the Author

Patricia A. Grenelle, PsyD, is a retired Forensic Psychologist who lives with her husband, Ed, a Retired US Army Major, and their Goldendoodle, JP, in the Sonoran Desert of Arizona. JP is her service animal for the diagnosis of complex post-traumatic stress disorder.

She aspires to reach people in her writing that may have experienced abuse and the controls of those who prey upon them. It is her goal to encourage people to live a more productive and happy life and she hopes that sharing her life has helped to accomplish that in some small way.

She encourages anyone who is touched by this book to begin helping to put a stop to childhood sexual abuse, rape, and trauma by supporting the organizations annotated in this work.

SubStack:@PatriciaGrenelle

https://PatriciaGrenelle.com

www.ingramcontent.com/pod-product-compliance
Lightning Source LLC
Chambersburg PA
CBHW051212120626
46547CB00013B/1322